REbel CoOK

REbel CoOK

BENDING THE RULES
FOR BRILLIANT FOOD

Simon Rimmer

Photography by Jason Lowe

CASSELL
ILLUSTRATED

This book is full of love for Ali, Flo and Hamish and is also for my mum and dad with love and thanks for lasagne and fried egg sandwiches x

First published in Great Britain in 2006 by Cassell Illustrated, a division of Octopus Publishing Group Limited 2-4 Heron Quays, London E14 4JP

A CIP catalogue record for this book is available from the British Library.

ISBN-13: 978-1-84403450-5
ISBN-10: 1-84403 450-X

10 9 8 7 6 5 4 3 2 1

Publishing Manager Anna Cheifetz
Edited by Joanne Wilson
Designed by John Round Design

Printed in China

CoNTents

inTROduction

I wish I could say that all the recipes in this book were learnt on my mother's knee and have been handed down from generation to generation, but if I did, I'd be lying. It's not that my mum isn't a good cook, she's brilliant – check out her lasagne on page 26 – and my dad can do a great Sunday lunch and the very best fried egg sandwich on the planet, it's just that I spent all my youth playing football and sulking, not cooking. Perhaps the start of the rebel in me ...

As you may or may not know, I taught myself to cook. I bought my restaurant in Manchester, Greens, in 1990 and couldn't afford to employ a chef and so, hey presto! – a chef was born. As a result, I tend to cook from instinct, rather than by learnt technique, and that's really what this book is all about. I've never felt the need to be bound by tradition and rules in the kitchen, and neither should you. Let's face it, if you come home from work and you fancy a bit of pasta for tea, but all you've got in the cupboard is chorizo and chickpeas, well you'll invent your own recipe of pasta with chorizo and chickpeas, you won't go searching for traditional Italian ingredients. So what you'll find in *Rebel Cook* is a collection of recipes that I've invented, stolen and adapted along the way.

One of the best things about being a chef is that fantastic moment when all the component parts of a recipe come together, it's all sitting on a plate and you take that first mouthful and think – oh yes! It's a winner! The other great thing is trying to recreate

a dish that you tasted somewhere and making it happen. They're both the product of experimentation and my recipes are a mixture of both. So, if you're not in a particularly rebellious frame of mind, you can try classic burrida, a little known version of cassoulet and a bakewell tart from the more 'traditional' side of the book and then, once you start to get carried away, devour delights such as gnocchi with duck ragout, wild boar and damson pie or chocolate fritters from the more rebellious side of the book … or should that be, the more rebellious side of my mind.

I hope you'll treat this book as a bit of a starting point for your own rebellion – if you don't like a bit of my recipe, feel free to alter it, make it better, personalise it – treat this book as your foodie ipod, make your own playlists and shuffle them all around.

I'm very lucky living and working in the North West of England, we have such fantastic produce and producers – cheese, black pudding, meat, fish, damsons. Many of these producers have become great friends and I urge you to support them and any local producers in your own area. I'd also love to cook for you at Greens, so if you do come and I'm not behind the stove that night, tell my team that Simon sent you!

I'm dead proud of this, my second book – I hope it inspires you to become a rebel cook, but most of all I hope you can make something yummy for your tea and impress your friends and family – there's no tricky recipes, my 8 year old Flo is a rebel cook already and as my 3-year-old, Hamish says 'my can did it'. Enjoy x

Braised chicken thighs in walnut sauce

Chicken thighs are dirt cheap and sooo tasty. This simple walnut sauce is great with the stronger taste of thigh as well as the fragrance of the pilaf rice. The meat looks lovely, so leave it in the serving dishes to let everyone dig in.

Serves (4)

olive oil for frying

50g/2oz butter

2 red onions, finely chopped

8 chicken thighs, skin on

1 bay leaf

handful fresh thyme

about 1 litre/1¾ pints chicken stock

2 egg yolks

200ml/7fl oz milk

a little grated nutmeg

150g/5oz walnuts, lightly crushed

salt and freshly ground black pepper

Pilaf

600ml/1 pint fresh chicken stock

250g/8oz long-grain rice

2 cloves

1 tsp nutmeg

1 garlic clove, crushed

30g/1½oz butter

handful chopped parsley

salt and freshly ground black pepper

Melt the oil and butter in a large frying pan over a medium heat, and cook the onions until soft and golden. Then remove them from the pan. Skewer the thighs with cocktail sticks if you want – they may unfurle a little if you don't – and brown them off, then add the onions, bay and thyme.

Cover with stock, then simmer for 30–40 minutes, until the chicken is cooked. Remove the chicken and keep warm. Strain the liquid into another pan, allow to bubble over a high heat until reduced by one-third. Meanwhile, whisk the egg yolks and milk together.

Turn the heat to low and add the egg mixture, stirring well. Keep stirring to thicken and do not let it boil. When fairly thick, add the nutmeg, walnuts and seasoning and simmer for 3 minutes.

To make the pilaf, bring the stock to the boil. Add the rice, cloves, nutmeg, salt and garlic. Stir well then cook, covered, on the hob for 15 minutes. Take off the heat, stir in the butter, adjust the seasoning and cover with a damp tea towel. Let it sit for 10 minutes before stirring in the parsley. Have the pilaf, chicken and sauce in separate serving bowls and let everyone serve themselves.

Lamb loin with baba-ganouch

This is a lovely dish combining the sweetness of lamb with the gutsy sharpness of the Indonesian-style baba-ganouch, a kind of aubergine puree. I love to serve it with slow-cooked beans in sweet almond and garlic butter.

Serves ②

2 aubergines

about a bunch each of mint, rosemary and parsley

2 x 175g/6oz lamb loins, with fat on and tied

extra virgin olive oil for frying

juice 1 lemon

4 garlic cloves, crushed

handful chopped parsley

1 tbsp tahini paste

pinch chilli powder

25g/1oz toasted, flaked almonds

75g/3oz unsalted butter

100g/3½oz runner beans, sliced and blanched

salt and freshly ground black pepper

Preheat the oven to 200°C/400°F/Gas Mark 6. Roast the aubergines in the oven for about 30 minutes, until the skins are well charred, and let them cool.

Meanwhile, chop the herbs and mix together well. Season the lamb and roll it in the herbs. Heat a little oil in a pan until smoking, then pop the lamb in the pan and seal on all sides to keep all the juices inside. Once sealed, cook in the hot oven for about 8 minutes. This will cook the meat to just medium. If you want it a little more cooked increase the cooking time, but not too much because it's much nicer pink.

To make the baba-ganouch, peel the cooled aubergines and chuck the flesh, lemon juice, half the garlic, the parsley, tahini and chilli into a food processor and blend until smooth. Once it's blended, adjust the seasoning.

Next, make the flavoured butter by pulsing the nuts, remaining garlic, butter and salt and pepper together. You only need about half the amount made. Wrap the rest in greaseproof paper: it will keep in a refrigerator for about a week and is delicious with white fish.

Finally, melt the butter gently, add the beans and cook over a low heat for about 5 minutes. To serve, spoon a little baba on the plate, slice the lamb into medallions and place on top of the baba. Serve the beans in a separate bowl.

Pork loin with figs, pomegranate and pistachios

The lovely, rich, treacly sauce in this dish is a real favourite of mine. It seems to bring out extra flavour from the meat and also has that 'What's in this beautiful sauce?' factor, which any insecure chef likes to hear. If you can get smoked pork loin, well that's even better.

Serves ④

2 x 350g/11½oz pork loins, each cut in 2

75g/3oz butter plus extra for frying and sealing

pinch cumin

75g/3oz soft dark brown sugar

125ml/4fl oz balsamic vinegar

6–8 figs, quartered

1 pomegranate, seeds only

zest ½ orange

150g/5oz shelled pistachios

salt and freshly ground black pepper

watercress to serve

Preheat the oven to 200°C/400°F/Gas Mark 6. Season the pork. On the hob, melt a little butter in a large ovenproof pan, add the cumin and seal the pork. Cook in the oven for about 12 minutes.

Melt the sugar and the rest of the butter in a heavy-bottomed saucepan until they begin to caramelize. Add the balsamic and stir really well to form a syrup. Take off the heat and immediately add the figs, pomegranate, orange zest and nuts, coating them all well in the syrup.

Slice the pork and serve on watercress with the sauce spooned over. This dish goes really well with small roasted spuds.

Beef rolls

Feel free to eat these for breakfast, lunch or dinner, as a starter or cold for a picnic. I think the descriptive word I'm looking for here is 'versatile'.

Serves ④

2 x 150g/5oz rump steaks, fat trimmed

100g/3½oz pecorino cheese, grated

75g/3oz fresh breadcrumbs

2 tbsp chopped parsley

75g/3oz pine nuts

2 tbsp finely chopped rosemary

olive oil for brushing

salt and freshly ground black pepper

green salad to serve

Cut each steak in half across the grain, then bash them out between clingfilm until about 2mm/⅟₁₆in thick. Season and lay them on a work surface.

Mix together the cheese, breadcrumbs, parsley, pine nuts, rosemary and salt and pepper. Spread the mix thinly on the four pieces of steak and roll up from the short side. Secure with cocktail sticks.

Season the outside, brush with olive oil and griddle for 3–4 minutes on each 'side'. Serve with a yummy salad.

Quail with chestnuts and calvados

I had never been the biggest fan of quail, but when I made this for the first time, I was a very happy chappy. I think then that this is quail for people who think they don't like quail – make this and be astounded.

Serves ④

8 small quail

2 dessert apples, peeled, cored and finely diced

1 onion, sliced

1 bay leaf

50ml/2fl oz Calvados

150g/5oz vacuum-packed chestnuts

about 400ml/14fl oz chicken stock

salt and freshly ground black pepper

Preheat the oven to 200°C/400°F/Gas Mark 6. Season the quail and stuff with the apples. Place in a roasting tin with the onion, bay leaf, Calvados and 4 of the chestnuts. Pour in enough stock to come a quarter of the way up the birds. Cover with foil and roast for 20 minutes. Remove the foil and cook for a further 10 minutes.

Transfer the birds to a warmed serving dish and keep warm; strain off the liquid into a saucepan, skim off any fat from the liquid, bring to the boil and reduce the liquid by half. Add the remaining chestnuts and warm through. Spoon the sauce over the birds, eat and enjoy.

Thai red duck curry

There are lots of ingredients here, but this recipe will make enough paste for about 20 portions of curry and it'll keep in the refrigerator for a good week. I adore Thai food, it's so fragrant and fresh and making your own paste makes it even more rewarding. It really is fantastic with duck.

Serves ④

Red curry paste

5 black peppercorns

1 tsp cumin seeds

1 tsp coriander seeds

5 red chillies, deseeded

2 shallots

1 tbsp crushed garlic

2.5cm/1in piece of ginger, peeled and chopped

3 lemon grass stalks

6 kaffir lime leaves

pinch cinnamon

pinch turmeric

splash Thai fish sauce

splash chilli oil

1 tbsp palm sugar

4 duck breasts

250ml/8fl oz chicken stock

400ml/14fl oz can coconut milk

8 spring onions, finely sliced

1 red pepper, deseeded and sliced

16 baby aubergines, halved (griddled for extra flavour, optional)

salt and freshly ground black pepper

cooked sticky rice, coriander and lime wedges to serve

To make the paste, dry-fry the peppercorns, cumin seeds and coriander seeds for about 5 minutes to release their flavour, then grind them in a pestle and mortar. Blend them together with all the remaining ingredients until smooth.

Score the skin of the duck, season with salt and place in a cold pan, on a medium heat. Keep tipping off the fat as it is released (you can keep it if you wish, to make a lovely stock for roasting potatoes in), and cook for 5 minutes, flip over and seal the other side. Remove the duck and keep warm.

Heat a good spoonful of paste in the pan and cook on a low heat until fragrant. Add the stock and coconut milk and bring to the boil. Slice the duck breasts, season and add them and the spring onions, pepper and aubergines and cook for 5 minutes or until the aubergines are soft. Serve with a mound of sticky rice, chopped coriander and lime wedges.

Pork with clams

This is a tasty tapas-style dish that, as with so many tapas, can be made bigger or smaller for a main course or a starter. I like this mid-ground taster kind of size, so your appetite's been woken up and you're left wanting more.

Serves (6)

500g/1lb boneless pork shoulder, cubed

olive oil for frying

2 onions, finely sliced

50g/2oz prosciutto

150g/5oz spicy chorizo

6 garlic cloves, crushed

1 large green pepper, deseeded and chopped

1 bay leaf

400g/13oz can tomatoes

75g/3oz tomato purée

225ml/7½fl oz white wine

100g/3½oz small clams

fresh coriander and sour cream to serve

In a large frying pan, brown the cubed meat all over, then remove and set aside. Very gently fry the onions, prosciutto, chorizo, garlic, pepper and bay leaf in the same pan for about 10 minutes until soft.

Now add the tomatoes, tomato purée and wine. Bring to the boil, then reduce to a simmer. Put the meat back in and cook for about 30 minutes until it is tender.

Just before serving, add the clams to the pan. Shake them around and cook for about 5 minutes until they open. Spoon into small bowls and top with coriander and sour cream.

Green chicken thighs

I can see the look on your face, 'Green chicken – gross!'. Well, what we do here is double-marinate the chicken, finishing it with a coriander marinade, which is green. In spite of the colour, you will never stop making these.

Serves ⑥

12 skinless chicken thighs

1 tbsp vegetable oil

3 tbsp white vinegar

2 garlic cloves, crushed

2.5cm/1in piece of ginger, peeled and finely chopped

salt

Chutney

4 chillies (Scotch bonnet chilli peppers are best if you can get them)

12 spring onions, chopped

1 bunch mint

1 large bunch fresh coriander

juice 3 limes

1 tsp sugar

salt and freshly ground black pepper

natural yogurt and salad to serve

Make 2–3 deep cuts into each chicken thigh. Combine the oil, vinegar, garlic, ginger and salt and rub well into the chicken. Put it in a bowl, cover and chill overnight.

To make the chutney, blend the chillies, spring onions, mint and coriander (stalks and all) until smooth in a food processor. Now add the lime juice, keeping the motor running, then add the sugar, salt and pepper.

Preheat the grill to medium-high heat. Just before cooking, rub the chutney into the chicken, then grill for about 20 minutes in total, turning occasionally.

Serve with natural yogurt and salad.

Chorizo with sherry

Tapas – yum-yum. We eat so much chorizo in our house and this is one of my favourite ways to eat it. It packs a great punch – spicy, crispy, rich and oily. Try this once and then you'll find a million things to use it for, if ever you get to the point where you don't just scoff it all straight away.

Serves just ①!

400g/13oz spicy chorizo
olive oil for frying
150ml/¼ pint dry sherry

Cut the chorizo into bite-sized bits. Heat the oil to smoking then fry the chorizo until it is crispy. Now add the sherry and reduce by half, then eat it all up!

Warm potato salad with garlic sausage

I'm using artistic licence calling this a salad, because it's really warm spuds with sausage and melting cheese and is fantastic winter comfort food.

Serves ④ hungry ones or ⑥ polite ones

700g/1lb 6oz new potatoes
100ml/3½fl oz white wine
225ml/7½fl oz chicken stock
100g/3½oz garlic sausage, cut into 1cm/½in thick slices
75g/3oz Gruyère cheese, cut into very small cubes
2 tsp each finely chopped tarragon, chives and chervil

Vinaigrette
1tbsp Dijon mustard
75ml/3fl oz white wine vinegar
100ml/3½fl oz extra virgin olive oil
salt and freshly ground black pepper

Preheat the oven to 180°C/350°F/Gas Mark 4. Cook the potatoes in boiling water until just soft. Drain and cut into thick slices. Bring the wine and stock to the boil in a pan and reduce by two-thirds. Remove from the heat, toss the spuds in the mix and leave for 10 minutes to infuse. Meanwhile, warm the sausage in the oven for 6 minutes. Drain off any excess liquid from the spuds and combine the sausage and spuds.

Whisk together the mustard and vinegar, then slowly add the oil and season. Pour this over the 'salad'. Add the cheese and herbs, toss together, and serve either in a big bowl or on individual plates.

Cassoulet

We normally think of cassoulet as a rich all-in-one casserole. Well, this is an equally traditional, but not so well-known, version that has the beans served separately. I use canned beans, to save time. A nice crisp sauvignon blanc is just what you need to cut through the delicious, rich flavours.

Serves ⑥

450g/14½oz lamb shoulder, cubed

oil for sealing

400g/13oz can haricot beans, drained and rinsed

225g/7½oz good-quality spicy, garlicy dried sausage

350g/11½oz can confit duck or goose

2 tomatoes, chopped

1 onion, stuck with 2 cloves

handful chopped parsley

100g/3½oz thick-sliced streaky bacon, chopped

2 garlic cloves, crushed

50g/2oz fresh breadcrumbs

Preheat the oven to 180°C/350°F/Gas Mark 4. On the hob, seal the lamb over a medium heat in a large ovenproof dish with a little oil. Add the beans, sausage, duck (or goose) confit, tomatoes, onion and parsley. Cover the ingredients with freshly boiled water, then cover and cook in the oven very slowly for 2 hours.

Add the bacon and garlic and cook for 1½ hours more. Remove the dish from the oven and transfer the beans and some of the cooking liquid to an ovenproof dish, top with the breadcrumbs and cook in the oven for 15 minutes (you could grill the dish if you prefer).

Serve the beans on a separate plate from the meat.

Rabbit with capers and anchovies

My favourite way to cook is to use great ingredients in simple dishes, and this is a fine example. If you're really short of time, you can even get away without marinating the rabbit: just toss it in flour and go for it.

Serves **4**

Marinade
50ml/2fl oz olive oil

525ml/17½fl oz dry white wine

2 garlic cloves, crushed

juice 1 lemon

1 onion, chopped

1 carrot, chopped

1 celery stick, chopped

2 bay leaves

fresh rosemary and parsley

salt and freshly ground black pepper

1.5kg/3lb rabbit, cut into about 8 pieces

seasoned plain flour for dusting

50ml/2fl oz olive oil

1 small hot chilli, deseeded and finely chopped

8 fresh anchovies in vinegar

75g/3oz salted capers, rinsed

2 garlic cloves, crushed

cooked new potatoes and cooked, shelled chestnuts to serve

Mix all the marinade ingredients together and marinate the rabbit overnight.

Preheat the oven to 180°C/350°F/Gas Mark 4. Pat the rabbit pieces dry, reserving the marinade, then toss in the seasoned flour. Heat the oil to smoking, chuck in the chilli and the rabbit and fry the meat to seal. Transfer the rabbit to an ovenproof dish and cook in the oven for about 25 minutes.

Meanwhile, chop the anchovies, capers and garlic. Place in a small pan with about a quarter of the reserved marinade. Bring to the boil and simmer for about 5 minutes. Pour over the rabbit and serve with buttered spuds and chestnuts.

Rolled, stuffed beef

If you invite me round for tea and want to cook something from the book, then this should be high on your list – beef, which I love, a tapenade-y filling, rich tomato sauce and a recipe that's a doddle to make, leaving plenty of time for a couple of glasses of Billecart Salmon Rosé champagne. The key to this dish is to get the steak nice and thin so it cooks quickly.

Serves ④

4 x 150g/5oz trimmed rump steaks

100g/3½oz canned anchovies

100g/3½oz green olives, pitted

75g/3oz sun-dried tomatoes in oil, drained

1 garlic clove

75g/3oz parsley, chopped

salt and freshly ground black pepper

Sauce

1 onion, finely chopped

olive oil for frying and thinning

1 garlic clove, chopped

750g/1½lb tomatoes, skinned, deseeded and chopped

chopped parsley and cooked long-grain rice to serve

Place the steak between layers of clingfilm and flatten until nice and thin. Season well.

Either finely chop the anchovies, olives, tomatoes, garlic and parsley, or pulse to a rough paste in a blender. Lay a spoonful of the paste over each steak, roll up and secure with a cocktail stick. Place in a lightly oiled baking dish.

Preheat the oven to 200°C/400°F/Gas Mark 6 and make the sauce. Gently fry the onion in a little of the oil until soft, but not coloured. Add the garlic, tomatoes and enough oil to give a saucy consistency. Spoon over the beef.

Roast in the oven for about 10 minutes until just cooked through and serve with buttery long-grain rice, stirred through with the chopped parsley.

My mum's lasagne

My mum, Angela Rimmer, is a fantastic cook and this is the best recipe for lasagne EVER! No béchamel, my mum uses cottage cheese and it is gorgeous. When you make this, make sure you say thanks to my mum. Love you, Mum xx

Serves 6–8

oil for frying

450g/14½oz lean minced beef

1 onion, finely chopped

1 red pepper, deseeded and finely chopped

1 green pepper, deseeded and finely chopped

150g/5oz button mushrooms, sliced

200g/7oz tomato purée

2 bay leaves

2 x 400g/13oz can chopped tomatoes

1 tsp each dried thyme, parsley and oregano

300g/10oz cottage cheese

150g/5oz grated mature Cheddar cheese

300g/10oz pasta sheets, dried or fresh (my mum says no pre-cook, dried is her choice)

salt and freshly ground black pepper

In a large frying pan, heat the oil and brown the mince, then set aside. Now gently fry the onion, peppers and mushrooms until soft. Pop the mince back in together with the tomato purée and bay leaves and cook for 5 minutes. Now add the tomatoes and herbs, bring to the boil, then simmer for at least 30 minutes and season well.

Preheat the oven to 180°C/350°F/Gas Mark 4. Grease a 25 x 20cm/10 x 8in baking dish and line the bottom with pasta. Fish out the bay leaves and spoon about one-third of the mix on to the pasta, then put blobs of cottage cheese (again about one-third) on top of the mince. Carry on for 2 more layers, finishing with meat, cottage cheese and then the Cheddar. Bake for about 45 minutes to 1 hour. At my mum's, we have this with salad and sometimes garlic bread.

Goat curry with rice and peas

You can make this curry with lamb or mutton, but if you can get goat meat, then it's worth it; try your local butcher and even supermarkets in some areas. My friends Sharon and Martin insist that you wash the meat in a little white vinegar and water before using to both tenderize and clean it.

Serves (8)

Curry

150ml/¼ pint vegetable oil

1kg/2lb goat meat, cubed

2 onions, finely chopped

65g/2½oz curry powder

1 tbsp dried chilli flakes

1 bay leaf

1 tsp ground allspice

400ml/14fl oz can coconut milk

400ml/14fl oz chicken stock

juice 2 limes

Rice and peas

50ml/2fl oz vegetable oil

1 onion, finely chopped

300g/10oz long-grain rice

400ml/14fl oz water

400ml/14fl oz coconut milk

400g/13oz can kidney beans, drained and rinsed

3 tbsp fresh thyme

salt and freshly ground black pepper

fresh coriander to serve

To make the curry, heat the oil in a large, heavy-bottomed pan, then brown the meat and remove. Now fry the onions until golden. Add the curry powder, chilli flakes, bay leaf, allspice and coconut milk. Cook for a couple of minutes, then put the meat back in, add enough of the stock to cover, then turn the heat right down and simmer for 2–4 hours until really tender. Just before serving, stir in the lime juice.

For the rice and peas, heat the oil in a large pan and fry the onion until soft, but not coloured. Now add the rice, stir well and add the water and coconut milk. Bring to the boil. Next, add the kidney beans and thyme and simmer, covered, for about 20 minutes until the rice is cooked. Season.

Serve a good spoonful of the rice with lots of curry and coriander, and a very, very chilly lager.

Jerk chicken and coconut rice in banana leaf

Jerk chicken is such a treat, deep-fried, spicy and only to be eaten with your fingers. But it has to be top quality spice. The chicken with sticky, coconut rice parcels, hot sauce and lager is a meal to be eaten on the sofa, watching telly, preferably footy with Liverpool winning.

Serves ⑥

Parcels

2 plantains

seasoned plain flour for rolling

vegetable oil for frying

225g/7½oz long-grain rice

450ml/¾ pint water

200g/7oz block creamed coconut, chopped

2 small red chillies, deseeded and sliced

6 pieces banana leaf, about 30cm x 20cm/12in x 8in

handful fresh coriander

12 chicken legs

good flat plateful jerk seasoning, at least 150g/5oz

vegetable oil for deep-frying

Jamaican hot sauce to serve

Slice the plantain pieces to pound-coin thickness (about 5mm/¼in) and roll in the seasoned flour. Fry the plantain in the oil, on both sides, in a large pan until crisp. Wash the rice and put in a pan with the water and creamed coconut. Bring to the boil and cook for about 10 minutes.

Take the pan off the heat and stir in the chillies and plantain slices. Divide between the pieces of banana leaf, lay some coriander on top, wrap them up and secure with a skewer. Steam the parcels in batches in a steamer, or over a large pan of boiling water, for 5 minutes.

For the chicken, simply roll in the seasoning and deep-fry for 8–10 minutes in a wok or deep-frier. (To see if the oil is up to temperature put a small bit of bread in, which should brown straight away.) Drain on kitchen paper. Serve a parcel of rice with chicken and hot sauce and some cold lager.

Rack of lamb with bean gratin

Rack of lamb has gone from being the restaurant fave to a dinner party must-do. I love to use salt marsh lamb, as it has a distinct, earthy flavour like no other. Ask your butcher to prepare the lamb 'French', which means a leaner trim and all the meat removed from the rib bones. Be sure to make the crust as the extra layer of flavour is well worth it.

Serves ④

Crust

25g/1oz each of chopped, fresh parsley, tarragon, rosemary and thyme

225g/7½oz fresh breadcrumbs

1 garlic clove, crushed

50ml/2fl oz olive oil

olive oil for frying

2 x 7-rib rack of lamb, preferably French-prepared

30g/1½oz Dijon mustard

salt and freshly ground black pepper

Beans

1 shallot, finely chopped

2 celery sticks, chopped

2 garlic cloves, crushed

1 carrot, finely chopped

2 x 400g/13oz can flageolet beans, drained and rinsed

125g/4oz crème frâiche

50g/2oz fresh breadcrumbs

100g/3½oz grated Parmesan

30g/1½oz melted butter

salt and freshly ground black pepper

gravy to serve

Make the crust by simply combining all the ingredients. Preheat the oven to 220°C/425°F/Gas Mark 7.

Heat some oil in a pan until nearly smoking. Season the racks, then cook until crisp and brown on both sides, about 7 minutes. Remove from the pan and brush with the mustard on the rounded, skinned side of the best end. Then press the crust on to the mustard and roast the lamb in the hot oven for about 20 minutes.

While the lamb is cooking, prepare the beans. Gently fry the shallot, celery, garlic and carrot until soft. Take off the heat, add the beans and fold in the crème frâiche. Season and transfer to a shallow casserole dish. Mix together the breadcrumbs, Parmesan and butter, then sprinkle over the beans.

Remove the meat from the oven and allow to rest for 20 minutes. Reduce the oven temperature to 200°C/400°F/Gas Mark 6. Cook the beans in the slightly cooler oven for 20 minutes.

Serve the lamb with the beans and some gravy.

Fiery Korean beef with white radish salad

A glorious hot, fiery salad, full of flavour: a little more raw in style than a Thai beef salad, but with similar fire. Serving rice with it means the neutral flavour takes out any painful chilli burn and rounds off the taste. Whenever I make it, there's always a clamour for the recipe … and a glass of cold water.

Serves ⑥

Marinade
1 garlic clove
1 tsp sugar
1 tsp salt
50ml/2fl oz soy sauce
1 tbsp sesame oil
1 tsp Chinese red-bean paste
35ml/1½fl oz water
35ml/1½fl oz sherry
1 tsp toasted sesame seeds
2 spring onions, finely chopped
1 tsp dried chilli flakes

1 kg/2 lb rump steak

Salad
2 cooking apples
2 mouli/white radish
juice 1 lemon
3 spring onions, finely sliced

Dressing
50ml/2fl oz light soy sauce
15ml/½fl oz sesame oil
50ml/2fl oz rice vinegar
15g/½oz sugar
5g/¼oz salt
15g/½oz sesame seeds
1 bird's eye chilli, finely chopped

steamed white rice to serve and coriander leaves to garnish

Make the marinade by crushing the garlic with the sugar and salt to make a paste, then combining this with all the other marinade ingredients. Slice the beef very thinly. Marinate the beef for at least 4 hours in half the marinade.

When ready, shake off any excess marinade and griddle the beef very quickly on each side: in, out – that fast.

To prepare the salad, peel and cut the apples and radishes into matchsticks, and soak in some cold water and the lemon juice for 10 minutes. Drain, then mix all the dressing ingredients together, then toss the drained radish, apple and finely sliced onions in the dressing.

To serve, sit the meat on a plate and then put the salad in a bowl, the remaining marinade (now a dip called bulgogi sauce) in another bowl and the rice in another bowl. Garnish with a little coriander.

Scouse

This really should be our national dish, even though it comes from Scandinavia. The name tends to be more associated with people from the best city in the world, rather than the dish. I know that loads of you will argue with my recipe, especially the Worcestershire sauce, but it's my book and that means it's right.

Serves ④–⑥

50g/2oz butter for buttering and melting

875g/1¾lb potatoes, sliced

875g/1¾lb shoulder lamb, cubed

2 carrots, sliced

2 onions, finely sliced

3 lambs' kidneys, cored, split and quartered

handful fresh thyme

1 bay leaf

splash Worcestershire sauce

575ml/18fl oz beef stock

salt and freshly ground black pepper

pickled beetroot to serve

Preheat the oven to 180°C/350°F/Gas Mark 4. Butter a casserole dish and line with a layer of spuds. Season well. Layer up the meat, carrots, onions, kidneys, herbs and seasoning. Finish with a layer of overlapping spuds.

Add the Worcestershire sauce to the stock and pour in enough to reach the bottom of the top layer of spuds. Brush the top with melted butter. Cover and cook in the oven for 2 hours.

Take off the lid and cook for 30 minutes more, to crisp the spuds.

Serve with pickled beetroot.

Roast goose with prune and chestnut stuffing

I was filming at Holly Tree Farm, where horses come up to say 'hello', pigs crave the attention of the camera and geese zoom out of their sheds like a scene from The Dambusters. I realised I've never written a simple guide to cooking a goose, a fatty bird that can disappoint, but won't, if cooked like this.

Serves all the family (at least ⑧)

1 leek, sliced

1 onion, quartered

6kg/12lb goose, with giblets

goose fat for roasting

1 tbsp cornflour

1kg/2lb potatoes, peeled and cut into large pieces

salt and freshly ground black pepper

Stuffing

450g/14½oz prunes

250ml/8fl oz port

30g/1½oz butter for frying

1 onion, finely chopped

6 celery sticks, chopped

2 garlic cloves, crushed

1kg/2lb vacuum-packed chestnuts

5 tbsp chopped flat-leaf parsley

Preheat the oven to 200°C/400°F/Gas Mark 6. Pop the leek and onion in the goose cavity and prick the skin all over. Rub in the seasoning. Rub a little extra goose fat over the legs and cover them well with foil. Line a deep roasting dish with more foil, enough to make a parcel for the goose. Sit the goose on a rack in the dish and wrap it loosely. Roast in the heated oven for about 15 minutes per 450g/14½oz plus an extra 20 minutes. (So this 6kg/12lb goose needs about 3½ hours.)

After an hour, baste the goose and make sure the legs aren't burning. For the last 45 minutes, cook uncovered. Rest for 20 minutes before serving. Meanwhile, boil the giblets in about 2.5 litres/4 pints water for 3 hours, then strain and thicken with a little cornflour, to make a yummy gravy. Par-boil the spuds.

Heat the goose fat to smoking in a roasting tin, then pop in the spuds, give them a good shake, season well and roast with the goose for 45 minutes, or until crisp (give 'em a shake or two every now and again).

For the stuffing, soak the prunes in the port for about 2 hours. Gently fry the onion, celery and garlic in the butter until soft. Chop the chestnuts and prunes, add them and the port to the pan and simmer for 30 minutes. Take off the heat, stir in the parsley and season. Re-heat for 10 minutes then serve the meat with roasties, gravy and vegetables of your choice.

Posh lamb biryani

I always thought biryani was a bit dull at all the curry houses, then a friend of mine cooked it properly for me. Layering up all the ingredients, then serving the meat separately is a complete taste revolution. If you want to, make your own curry sauce, but I think the shops do some corkers these days.

Serves ④–⑥

Marinade
2 garlic cloves, crushed
5cm/2in piece of ginger, grated
pinch cayenne pepper
4 tsp paprika
4 tsp ground cumin
pinch ground cloves
salt

1kg/2lb lamb loin, cut into 3.5cm/1½in chunks
6 red chillies, deseeded and chopped
50g/2oz cashew nuts
oil for frying
500g/1lb mushrooms, sliced
2 garlic cloves, crushed
2.5cm/1in piece of ginger, finely chopped
100g/3½oz natural yogurt
1 tbsp garam masala
250g/8oz biryani rice, washed and soaked for 30 minutes, then drained
pinch turmeric
½ onion, sliced
25g/1oz butter for greasing
2 bay leaves
juice 1 lime
50ml/2fl oz rosewater
50ml/2fl oz vegetable oil
pinch saffron, dissolved in 50ml/2fl oz milk
melted butter with the juice of 1 lemon
handful chopped mint
salt and freshly ground black pepper
2 tbsp medium curry sauce to serve

Mix the marinade ingredients together and rub into the lamb chunks. Chill overnight. Allow the lamb to get up to room temperature, then thread 2–3 chunks on to long wooden skewers. Position them at the end so they look like lamb lollies.

Make a paste of the chillies and nuts in a blender, then fry in a little oil gently for 5 minutes. Add the mushrooms, garlic, ginger, yogurt, garam masala and seasoning. Fry gently for 5 minutes.

In a separate pan, fry the rice in a little oil for about 3 minutes. Add just enough water to cover, season, add the turmeric and cook until done, about 30 minutes. Lay out on a tray to dry a little.

Meanwhile, preheat the oven to 180°C/350°F/Gas Mark 4. Fry the onion until golden and crisp. Grease either individual ovenproof dishes or one large one with butter, then sit the bay leaves on the bottom. Now layer up rice, the mushroom mix, onion and a splash of the lime juice and rosewater. Repeat, then pour over the saffron milk. Cover with foil and cook in the oven for 30 minutes.

When the biryani is done, grill the lamb for about 4 minutes, turning regularly and basting with the butter and lemon juice. Serve wedges of the biryani with the rice, sprinle over the mint and drizzle with some curry sauce, heated through with a little stock if you wish.

Turkey mussaman cur

Roast turkey on Christmas Day, cold turkey with chips on Boxing Day. The good news is you can have it in this delicious Burmese-style mussaman curry for the rest of the year.

Serves ⑥

Paste

12 chillies, deseeded and chopped

3 shallots, sliced

5 garlic cloves, crushed

2 lemon grass stalks, chopped

2.5cm/1in piece of ginger, peeled and chopped

1 tsp cumin seeds

1 tbsp coriander seeds

2 cloves

6 peppercorns

1 tsp shrimp paste

1 tsp sugar

35ml/1½fl oz vegetable oil plus a little for frying

500g/1lb diced turkey

250ml/8fl oz creamed coconut

400ml/14fl oz can coconut milk

splash Thai fish sauce

1 tbsp palm sugar

4 tbsp tamarind paste

1 cinnamon stick

1 onion, roughly chopped

100g/3½oz streaky bacon, cooked and roughly chopped

225g/7½oz cooked potatoes

jasmine rice and handful roasted peanuts to serve

To make the paste, dry-fry all the ingredients except the shrimp paste, sugar and oil for 5–6 minutes. Then blend with the shrimp paste, sugar and oil in a bowl until smooth.

Seal the turkey in a little hot oil in the still hot pan, remove from the pan and gently fry the paste. Cook the paste for a few minutes until it becomes fragrant, then add the creamed coconut a little at a time. Next add the coconut milk and bring to the boil. Add the fish sauce, palm sugar, tamarind paste, cinnamon, onion, bacon and turkey. Cook for 15 minutes. Finally add the cooked spuds, warm through and serve with the rice and peanuts.

Lemon and garlic roast lamb

The joy of this Sunday lunch winner is that everything gets cooked in one pot, so it's hassle free. I wish I had more time to sit and have a family roast as it's one of my favourite occasions – all the clan around the table, squabbling, gossiping and seeing who can have the last word … these days it tends to be Hamish, and he's not even 3.

Serves ⑥

1.75kg/3½lb leg lamb

5 garlic cloves, sliced thinly

300g/10oz cherry tomatoes

2 onions, finely sliced

500g/1lb small potatoes

2 bulbs garlic, cut in half across the centre

200ml/7fl oz white wine

sea salt

Marinade

juice 2 lemons

100ml/3½fl oz olive oil

1 tbsp dried oregano

Make a load of fine slits in the lamb. Make the marinade by mixing together the lemon juice, oil and oregano. Now rub this into the lamb. Next press the sliced garlic into the slits, then sprinkle with sea salt. Marinate for at least 2 hours in the refrigerator.

Preheat the oven to 200°C/400°F/Gas Mark 6. Transfer the lamb into a roasting dish, then toss the tomatoes, onions, spuds and garlic heads in the marinade. Arrange the veggies around the lamb and roast in a hot oven for 1 hour. Halfway through, pour over the wine.

After an hour take out of the oven, cover with foil to keep warm and rest for about 15 minutes before serving.

Steak, shoestring fries and rosewater and chilli sauce

I think this is one of the most rewarding ways to eat steak – thick-cut rump for masses of flavour, shoestring fries that are impossible to leave and this wicked little chilli sauce with smoky ancho chillies. Bring it on!

Serves ②

Sauce

100ml/3½fl oz olive oil

65g/2½oz stale ciabatta, cubed

2 garlic cloves, chopped

2 Scotch bonnet chillies, chopped

1 tbsp dried ancho chillies, chopped

35ml/1½fl oz red wine

35ml/1½fl oz rosewater

150g/5oz pistachios

1 tbsp red wine vinegar

Fries

225g/7½oz potatoes, preferably maris piper

oil for deep-frying and frying

2 x thick-cut rump steaks (200g/7oz each)

50g/2oz butter

salt and freshly ground black pepper

First make the sauce. Heat the oil, then fry the bread until golden and take out of the pan. Now fry the garlic and fresh chillies until soft. Then blend with the rest of the ingredients, including the bread, until smooth, but still a little chunky, if you know what I mean.

To make the fries, peel the spuds, then grate on a mandolin at its thinnest setting, or hand cut very, very fine (but don't use a grater or the spuds will be charred scraps). Pop them in cold water for about 30 minutes – this will break down the starch and make 'em lovely and crisp.

After 30 minutes, take them out of the water, pat dry and deep-fry for about 2 minutes until crisp and golden. Scoop out of the oil, drain on kitchen paper and sprinkle with a little salt.

Meanwhile, season the steak with plenty of salt and pepper. Heat some oil until smoking, turn the heat down just a smidgen and pop in the steak. Cook for about 2 minutes on each side for medium-rare. Serve the steak topped with a slice of cold butter, then some sauce in a separate bowl and a large pile of dangerously naughty fries.

Yummy pork meatballs

If the only way you've eaten meatballs is with pasta, covered in tomato sauce, then be prepared for a taste revolution. These chaps are fragrant, juicy and are a fab starter. They also work really well without the noodles and watercress, if you make them tiny and serve them as canapés at that next groovy party you're planning.

Serves ④

Meatballs

450g/14½oz minced pork

5 garlic cloves, chopped

1 lemon grass stalk, finely chopped

4 spring onions, chopped

1 tbsp chopped fresh coriander

2 tbsp Thai red curry paste

juice 1 lime

1 tbsp fish sauce

1 egg

vegetable oil for grilling

salt and freshly ground black pepper

Cucumber relish

4 tbsp rice vinegar

4 tbsp water

50g/2oz sugar

1 garlic clove, finely sliced

1 cucumber, quartered and sliced

4 shallots, finely sliced

2.5cm/1in piece of ginger, peeled and finely chopped

200g/7oz fine egg noodles, cooked, bunch watercress and fresh coriander leaves to garnish

To make the meatballs, simply combine all the ingredients, season and mould into small balls. You should get about 12–16. Lay them on a baking tray and grill under a preheated medium grill for about 6–8 minutes, turning and brushing with a little oil as they brown.

To make the cucumber relish, bring the vinegar, water and sugar to the boil in a small pan. Stir until the sugar dissolves and becomes a little syrupy. Take off the heat and let it cool. Now stir in the rest of the ingredients.

To serve, toss the noodles and watercress in the relish, divide into 4 and top with the meatballs and chopped coriander leaves.

Beef stroganoff pie

I can remember having beef strog as a kid and thinking it was rubbish, then I had it as a grown-up in a grotty pub ... and still thought it was rubbish. Then I had to cook it on telly and thought 'I hate beef strog ... it's rubbish', but for the first time I researched it, cooked it, adjusted it and now, guess what? I love it. I also really love pies, so it's a match made in heaven.

Makes ④ pies

300g/10oz fillet steak, trimmed

75g/3oz smoked paprika

vegetable oil for frying

50g/2oz butter for frying

1 onion, sliced

50g/2oz button mushrooms, sliced

50g/2oz Portobello (or field) mushrooms, sliced

1 garlic clove, crushed

50ml/2fl oz brandy

150ml/¼ pint fresh beef stock

125ml/4fl oz soured cream

4 pieces of ready-rolled puff pastry, cut about 1.5cm/¾in wider than each dish (or 1 big piece done in the same way)

1 beaten egg, to glaze

salt and freshly ground black pepper

pickled red cabbage or beetroot, to serve

Cut the steak into strips across the grain. Dust with some of the paprika and season. Heat the oil in a pan to smoking and fry the beef quickly, until cooked through, remove and keep warm.

Melt the butter in the same pan, and cook the onion until soft and slightly golden. Add the sliced mushrooms and garlic and cook for a couple of minutes to soften. Add the brandy and flame (don't worry if it doesn't flame, cooking it will still get rid of the alcohol). Add the stock, bring to the boil and reduce by half. Add the soured cream and remaining paprika and reduce to the consistency of thick double cream. Pop the beef back in the pan to warm through and check the seasoning.

Preheat the oven to 200°C/400°F/Gas Mark 6. Divide the mixture between individual 11cm/4½in deep pie dishes or soufflé dishes. Brush some beaten egg around the top outside edges, then press the lids on and brush with lots of egg. Cut out a little vent in each for the steam and cook for about 10–15 minutes until the pie tops are crisp and golden. I reckon pickled red cabbage or beetroot go wonderfully well with these fellas.

Pork loin with prunes

I'm always excited by different taste sensations, and this is wonderful, sweet, soft pork sitting on top of a rich, mysterious sauce. For those in a romantic mood it would make a good seduction meal; simply halve the quantity of meat.

Serves ④

200g/7oz prunes

enough strong Assam tea to cover the prunes

1¼ tbsp ground coriander

1 tbsp ground cinnamon

4 x 200g/7oz pork loin fillet

olive oil for frying and drizzling

½ onion, finely chopped

6 tomatoes, peeled and chopped

1 tsp sugar

500g/1lb baby spinach

125ml/4fl oz extra virgin olive oil for the sauce

salt and freshly ground black pepper

Greek yogurt to serve

Soak the prunes in the tea overnight (or for at least 2 hours). Drain, and reserve a little of the tea.

Preheat the oven to 200°C/400°F/Gas Mark 6. Mix 1 tablespoon of the ground coriander with the cinnamon. Season the pork and rub with the spices. Heat a little oil in an ovenproof pan and seal the meat on all sides. Transfer to the oven and drizzle with a little oil. Cook in the oven for 12–15 minutes. Rest for 10 minutes, then cut into thick slices.

Gently fry the onion until soft, add the tomatoes, prunes, remaining ground coriander and sugar plus the reserved tea. Cook for about 5 minutes.

Next, mix in the spinach, some seasoning and the extra virgin olive oil. Spoon some sauce on to each plate and top with the sliced pork. Serve with Greek yogurt on the side.

Quebec-style duck with apple and banana

Once you get over the 'yuk' factor of syrup with savoury things, you'll be hugely surprised at how delicious it can be, but be careful when you're experimenting as maple syrup with beans on toast is just wrong. With duck and other fatty foods, such as salmon, it can be simply divine.

Serves ④

4 duck breasts

2 cooking apples, cut into 3mm/⅛in slices

3 shallots, sliced

1 bay leaf

handful fresh thyme

100ml/3½fl oz cider vinegar

300ml/½ pint chicken stock

100ml/3½fl oz pure maple syrup

2 small bananas, sliced

15g/½oz cold butter

salt and freshly ground black pepper

Score the skin on the duck breasts, season, then put into a cold pan with no oil. Turn on the heat and cook for about 5 minutes over a medium heat, to crisp up the breasts. Flip over and seal the other side, then take them out of the pan, allowing the fat to drip back in.

Now stir in the apples, shallots, bay, thyme, salt and pepper and cook for 3 minutes in the duck fat. Turn up the heat and add the vinegar, bring to the boil and reduce the liquid to almost nothing.

Next, add the stock and the maple syrup and bring to the boil. Turn the heat right down, return the duck to the pan and cook for about 8 minutes. Take the duck breasts and the apples out and reduce the sauce by about one-third.

Now throw in the bananas and whisk in the butter. To serve, pour the sauce over the sliced breasts and the apple.

Tandoori lamb chops

Never mind the barbie, I have a dream of owning my own tandoor and being able to cook a whole world of clay-oven dishes. Now that would be amazing. These chops are delicious simply grilled, but make sure you have the grill really hot before they go under.

Serves 4

Marinade
100ml/3½fl oz natural yogurt

juice 1 lime

5 garlic cloves, crushed

2.5cm/1in piece of ginger, peeled and grated

1 tsp cumin

1 tbsp ground coriander

1 tsp garam masala

pinch paprika

salt

Mint and coriander dip
3 green chillies, deseeded

6 spring onions

large bunch coriander

large handful mint

juice 2 limes

1 tsp sugar

300ml/½ pint natural yogurt

salt and freshly ground black pepper

400g/13oz lamb chops, about 8

butter and lemon juice, for grilling

Mix the yogurt and other marinade ingredients together. Put a few slashes across the lamb chops, then cover them well with the marinade and chill for 12 hours.

To make the dip, blend the chillies, spring onions, coriander, mint, lime juice, sugar and salt and pepper, then combine with the yogurt.

Shake any excess marinade off the chops, then grill under a hot grill for 8–10 minutes, turning once and basting with lemon and butter. Serve the piping hot chops with the dip.

Mozzarella with anchovy

I was never a fan of the deep-fried-Brie thing in the '80s. This, though, is impossible to resist. Creamy mozzarella with salty anchovies, and it's fried! Oh, this is soooo bad for you. But it is only a starter, so that's ok.

Serves (6)

450g/14½oz buffalo mozzarella, torn into pieces, about 50g/2oz each

seasoned plain flour for rolling

2 eggs, beaten

fresh breadcrumbs, for rolling

200ml/7fl oz olive oil for frying

Anchovy sauce

250ml/8fl oz extra virgin olive oil

10 canned anchovies, finely chopped

8 plum tomatoes, skinned, deseeded and finely chopped

handful chopped parsley

Thread 2 pieces of cheese on to a wooden skewer. Repeat until all the cheese is used up. Now roll in flour, then egg, then breadcrumbs.

Get the oil to almost smoking hot. Then 'medium fry' – neither deep nor shallow – turning regularly until they are crisp and brown. Drain on kitchen paper.

For the sauce, warm the oil, then drop in the anchovies and work them with a wooden spoon until they almost dissolve. Take off the heat and stir in the tomatoes and parsley.

Serve each skewer with some sauce drizzled over the top.

Smoked salmon hash

Going out for brunch has never really caught on in Britain, which is a shame as I would love to eat this in a fab diner/restaurant with lots of coffee. Maybe I should move to New York?

Serves ④

100g/3½oz butter

½ onion, finely sliced

500g/1lb new potatoes, cooked

1 tbsp chopped dill

175g/6oz smoked salmon, finely sliced

8 rashers good-quality, dry-cured smoked back bacon

4 eggs

3–4 tbsp Italian dressing (see recipe on page 118, but substitute oregano for lavender)

salt and freshly ground black pepper

Melt the butter in a large frying pan. Fry the onion until soft, add the spuds and cook until they begin to break down. Add the dill and smoked salmon and season well.

Meanwhile, grill the bacon until crispy and poach the eggs, preferably in an old-style poacher. For each serving, spoon half the spud mix on to a plate, sit 2 rashers of bacon alongside, then the egg and top with some dressing.

Sushi stuffed baby squid

This combination of light baby squid with delicious, rich brown shrimp is unbelievable. Stick these on the barbie in the summer for a really fantastic, smoky flavour.

Serves ④

125g/4oz sushi rice, cooked

25ml/1fl oz rice vinegar

75g/3oz brown shrimps, (buy these cooked and shelled)

1 tbsp chopped coriander

zest 1 lime

8 cleaned baby squid

oil, for grilling

salt and freshly ground black pepper

watercress, to serve

Marinade
juice 2 limes

100ml/3½fl oz light soy sauce

dash Thai fish sauce

handful chopped coriander

1 red chilli, deseeded and chopped

Dressing
1 tbsp wasabi paste

100ml/3½fl oz vegetable oil

dash sesame oil

dash Thai fish sauce

35ml/1½fl oz rice vinegar

Season the rice and add the vinegar, shrimps, coriander and lime zest. Now stuff the rice into the squid – you really need to pack it in.

Make the marinade by mixing all the ingredients together and place the squid in it for about an hour. Shake off any excess, rub with oil and griddle for a minute on each side.

Meanwhile, make the dressing by whisking together all the ingredients. Serve with watercress, and the dressing poured all over.

John Dory with gratin potato

Also known as Saint-pierre a la ménagère, this is a dish you must make now. It is a simple, tasty dish that's a joy to eat and really easy to make. John Dory is such an underrated fish in this country. If you've never had it, or not had it for a while, now is your big moment.

Serves ②

700g/1lb 6oz waxy potatoes, thinly sliced

2 x 700g/1lb 6oz John Dory, cleaned

75g/3oz butter, melted plus a little for greasing

125ml/4fl oz white wine

salt and freshly ground black pepper

chopped flat-leaf parsley and fresh, cooked green beans to serve

Preheat the oven to 180°C/350°F/Gas Mark 4. Blanch the spud slices for 2 minutes, refresh and drain well.

Butter an ovenproof dish large enough to hold the fish. Put a thin layer of spuds on the bottom. Season well and pour half the butter over. Lay the fish on top, drizzle with more butter and cover with the rest of the spuds. Season again, add the rest of the butter and the wine.

Cook in the oven for 30 minutes, basting frequently with the juices. Finish off by browning under the grill.

Chilli and lime prawns

I like to serve these as a starter in canapé-form, as grilling them with the shells on makes them ideal finger food. Feel free to up the chilli factor if you dare.

Serves ⑥

450g/14½oz tiger prawns, shells on

2 garlic cloves, crushed

juice and zest 1 lime

1 green chilli, very finely chopped (go on, leave the seeds in)

3 tbsp coriander stalk, chopped

30g/1½oz butter, melted

30g/1½oz olive oil

salt and freshly ground black pepper

Preheat the grill. Slice the prawns in half down the back, leaving the shell on. Mix together all the other ingredients and toss the prawns in this.

Transfer to an ovenproof dish and grill, flesh side up, for 2–3 minutes. Enjoy!

Baked mackerel with gooseberries

Mackerel is much-underrated. It's a lovely oily fish, with a strong taste, which means it can handle a big flavour. This sort of savoury gooseberry dish started life as a filling for a savoury cobbler, but I didn't make it as I'd got myself a bit of mackerel for tea, and I thought it'd go well. It did.

Serves ④

olive oil for greasing

4 mackerel, filleted

juice and zest 2 limes

salt and freshly ground black pepper

marjoram leaves

watercress to garnish

Sauce

50g/2oz butter

250g/8oz onion, finely chopped

250g/8oz gooseberries, topped and tailed

25g/1oz caster sugar

juice and zest 1 lime

handful fresh chopped marjoram

Grease an ovenproof dish and lay the fish in it, in a single layer, season, pour over the lime juice and zest and marinate for at least a couple of hours.

Preheat the oven to 200°C/400°F/Gas Mark 6 and prepare the sauce. Melt the butter in a saucepan, then fry the onions in butter until nice and soft. Add the gooseberries, sugar and lime and cook for 10–15 minutes until they begin to break down, then season and add the marjoram. Check the taste, you may want a little more sugar.

Meanwhile, scatter the fish with marjoram and bake in the oven for 10 minutes. Serve the fish with a spoonful of the gooseberry sauce, and garnish with watercress.

Haddock, patatas bravas, chorizo and rarebit

Cooked with potato, chorizo is the ultimate comfort food...well not quite, if you then sit a piece of juicy haddock, topped with sharp, tangy rarebit on the spuds and neck a very cold bottle of San Miguel, quite frankly I'm in the mood to sing 'Y Viva Espana' clutching a straw donkey.

Serves ① ⓪

Patatas bravas

6–8 large baking potatoes, peeled and cut into 2.5 cm/ 1 in cubes

olive oil for roasting

4 garlic cloves, crushed

2 x 400g/13oz cans chopped tomatoes

2 small red chillies, deseeded and chopped

1 tsp paprika

300g/10oz spicy chorizo (not pre-sliced), chopped into bite-sized pieces

loads of chopped parsley

10 x 150g/5oz haddock fillets (ask your fishmonger for fillets of the same shape and size, about a 10 x 7cm/4 x 3in rectangle)

juice 1 lemon

400g/13oz grated mature Cheddar or Manchego cheese

25g/1oz Dijon mustard

2 eggs, beaten

salt and freshly ground black pepper

I prefer making the bravas the day before and re-heating them: this allows the flavours to infuse into the spuds, making them even more tasty. To re-heat, pour some more oil over the top and warm through. To make them, preheat the oven to 200°C/400°F/Gas Mark 6. Discard the end and side bits of the spuds, so you're left with just the cubes, which look prettier.

Meanwhile, pour a big load of oil into your biggest roasting tin, so it's 2 cm/1in deep, and put it into the hot oven, until it smokes, then add the spuds, shake 'em around and season really well. After 10 minutes, shake again and add the crushed garlic, tomatoes, chillies, paprika and chorizo. After 30 minutes they should be crispy on the outside and oily, soft and spicy on the inside. Adjust the seasoning, add more oil if they're a little bit dry and fold in the parsley.

For the fish, lightly oil another roasting dish and lay all the fish in it. Season lightly and squeeze a touch of lemon juice on top. To make the rarebit, just combine the cheese, mustard, seasoning and beaten egg. Divide the mix into 10 and mould it into squares to fit on the top of the fish. Don't worry if it looks a bit sloppy: the egg will set it. Press them on to the fish, then roast for about 15 minutes in the oven, still at 200°C/400°F/Gas Mark 6, until the cheese browns and the fish is cooked. To serve, press a spoonful of bravas into a 10cm/4in ring, then sit the haddock on top.

Mussels and clams with pancetta

This is a very simple dish with a really intense flavour. It tastes magnificent with a load of crusty bread and a fruity glass of red, maybe a Brouilly.

Serves (6)

200g/7oz pancetta, cut into lardons

2 onions, finely chopped

2 garlic cloves, crushed

1 each of red, green and yellow peppers, deseeded and finely chopped

200ml/7fl oz white wine

300ml/½ pint fish stock

750g/1½lb mussels, scrubbed and beards removed

250g/8oz clams, scrubbed

2 tbsp red wine vinegar

1 tbsp fresh oregano

salt and freshly ground black pepper

shaved Parmesan cheese to serve

Fry the pancetta until crisp and remove from the pan. Using the bacon fat, fry the onion and garlic until soft. Now add the peppers and do the same.

Add the wine, bring to the boil and reduce to almost nothing. Now add the stock and return to the boil. Throw in the mussels and clams. Cover and cook for about 4 minutes over a high heat, giving the shellfish a good shake.

Take off the heat and discard any unopened shells. Stir in the vinegar, oregano and seasoning. Serve in 6 bowls and top with shaved Parmesan.

Salmon parcels

There's a scrummy Russian dish called Koulibiac, which is a kind of salmon and rice puff-pastry roll, and these parcels are similar in taste. As you may have noticed, I like individual things. It stops arguments about who got the biggest piece.

Serves ⑥

Filling

65g/2½oz basmati rice

pinch turmeric

butter for frying

1 onion, finely chopped

200g/7oz brown cap mushrooms, sliced

625g/1¼lb salmon, cooked and flaked

1 tbsp each chopped parsley and tarragon

2 eggs, hard-boiled and chopped

salt and freshly ground black pepper

500g/1lb ready-rolled puff pastry

1 egg, beaten, to glaze

sesame seeds to sprinkle

rocket leaves and pickled beetroot to serve

First make the filling. Cook the rice with the turmeric until just done, then drain. Melt the butter in a large frying pan, then gently fry the onion and mushrooms until soft. Stir in the rice, salmon, herbs, eggs and seasoning.

Roll out the pastry and cut into 6 x 15cm/6in squares. Place a good mound of the filling (about 150g/5oz) in the middle and wrap up tightly in a ball. Chill for 30 minutes.

Meanwhile preheat the oven to 200°C/400°F/Gas Mark 6. Brush the parcels with beaten egg, sprinkle with sesame seeds and cook for 30 minutes until crisp and golden. Serve with rocket leaves and pickled beetroot.

Burrida

This Spanish fish stew is such a magnificent dish. Make it for your friends, let them dig in and then lap up all the praise. It packs a real fishy flavour and you have to have seconds. Don't be put off by the fish heads, they really give a deep, rich flavour. Just imagining this dish makes me want to cook it right away.

Serves ⑥–⑧

Stock

butter for frying
50g/ 2oz shallots
1 leek, chopped
1 carrot, chopped
½ fennel bulb, chopped
2 celery sticks, chopped
30g/1½oz tomato purée
4 tomatoes
175ml/ 6fl oz white wine
50ml/2fl oz brandy
400g/13oz fish heads, eg. cod or bass
900ml/1½ pints fish stock
2 garlic cloves
1 bay leaf
sprig tarragon
pinch cayenne pepper
1 tbsp smoked paprika
400g/13oz assorted fish and shellfish such as salmon, cod, clams
12 new potatoes, cooked
2 carrots, sliced and cooked
100g/3½oz fine beans, chopped and cooked
handful parsley, chopped
juice 1 lemon
splash double cream
salt and freshly ground black pepper

crusty bread and garlic mayonnaise to serve

First make the stock. Melt the butter over a low heat and cook the shallots, leek, carrot, fennel and celery for 10 minutes until soft. Next, add the tomato purée, tomatoes, white wine and brandy. Bring to simmering point and continue cooking to reduce by half.

Add the fish heads and cook for 5 minutes, then add the stock, garlic, herbs and spices and cook for a further 40 minutes.

Blitz it in a food processor, fish heads and all, and pass first through a broad sieve, then a fine sieve. Really push the mix through the sieves to keep as much flavour as possible in the liquid. Discard the contents of the sieves.

Put the mixture back in the pan, bring to the boil, add the fish and vegetables. When it is cooked – no more than 5 minutes depending on your choice of fish – add some chopped parsley and the lemon juice and finish with a little cream. Serve with crusty bread and garlic mayonnaise.

Sea bass with potato rosti

The combination of fish and potato is one of the best in the world, I reckon I could do a book just about that combo. Try this one for your tea one night – the king of fish (also known as sea bass) looks so majestic on his rosti throne with his adoring subjects from the kingdom of salsa at his feet ... I need a drink.

Serves ④

2 large baking potatoes
3 finely sliced spring onions
clove crushed garlic

Salsa
150g/5oz smoked bacon lardons
1 small birds eye chilli, deseeded
about 20 cherry tomatoes, cut into quarters
1 tbsp chopped coriander
½ ripe avocado, cut into small cubes
1 tbsp sherry vinegar
4 tbsp extra virgin olive oil

4 x 150g/5oz sea bass fillets
olive oil for frying
salt and freshly ground black pepper

Boil the spuds in their jackets for 7 minutes, then drain and allow to cool a little. Peel and grate them coarsely, then add the onion, garlic and lots of seasoning.

Mould into 'rostis', chill for 20 minutes, then fry over a medium heat for 4 minutes each side until crisp and golden. Drain them on kitchen paper and keep warm.

For the salsa, fry the bacon until crispy, then simply combine with all the other ingredients (although you should leave the avocado until just before serving).

Preheat the oven to 200°C/400°F/Gas Mark 6. For the fish, season well and fry in the oil for 2 minutes, skin side down, then flip over and pop in the oven for 2 minutes.

To serve, sit a piece of yummy bass on top of a rosti and spoon over some refreshing salsa.

Alternative fish and chips

Let me introduce you to the deliciousness that is the dab. A relative of the plaice, it is sweeter, smaller and, in my opinion, tastier. It's also a fair bit cheaper. Because of its sweetness, I think the coconut crumb is just yummy with it, and it makes me think exotic. So, how about a mango 'ketchup'? If this is all too much, just wrap it all up in newspaper with the sweet potato chips, take it away and tuck in.

Serves ④–⑥

100g/3½oz fresh breadcrumbs

100g/3½oz desiccated coconut

1kg/2lb dab fillets, about 125g/4oz each

100g/3½oz plain flour

2 eggs, beaten

oil for frying

salt and freshly ground black pepper

Sauce

2 mangoes, flesh only

30g/1½oz soft dark brown sugar

30g/1½oz basil

1 garlic clove

50ml/2fl oz white wine

1 bird's eye chilli, deseeded

splash light soy sauce (optional)

salt and freshly ground black pepper

Chips

500g/1lb golden sweet potatoes

salt and cayenne pepper

vegetable oil for deep frying

Combine the breadcrumbs and coconut. Season the fish, then roll in the flour, followed by the egg and finally the crumb and coconut mix. Fry each fillet for a couple of minutes on each side. Don't overcrowd the pan, as this will stop the dabs cooking.

To make the sauce, simply blend all the ingredients until nice and smooth. Try using a little light soy in place of salt: it's fab.

When making the chips, it is time to watch your fingers: slice the peeled sweet spuds on the finest setting of a mandolin as if you were making shoestring fries. Pop them in water for 10 minutes.

Now simply drain, pat dry and deep-fry in a deep frier, wok or pan for about 45 seconds until crisp. Take them out, drain on kitchen paper and dust with a mix of salt and cayenne.

Serve the fish topped with fries and, if you wish, put the sauce in a sauce bottle and use it like a weird kind of ketchup.

Monkfish and artichokes

There are some dishes I think should be in everyone's repertoire, and this is definitely one of them. Monkfish is lovely and meaty: combine this with tomatoes and butter and spuds and make it all in the same pan and you've got a winner. Did I mention it's delicious? Use up any left-over butter on hot, toasted bagels.

Serves (4)

Flavoured butter

250g/8oz butter

1 garlic clove, crushed

100g/3½oz sun-dried tomatoes, in oil

salt and fresh ground black pepper

200g/7oz artichoke hearts (canned)

oil for brushing

400g/13oz trimmed monkfish tails

seasoned plain flour for dredging

juice 1 lemon

good handful cherry tomatoes

300g/10oz cooked new potatoes

handful chopped parsley

salt and freshly ground black pepper

First make the flavoured butter. Soften the butter, then blitz with black pepper, garlic and tomatoes until smooth. Form into a sausage shape, wrap it up in greaseproof paper and chill: overnight is good.

Cut the chokes in half, brush with oil and griddle until charred on each side. Cut the fish into goujons, then dredge them in seasoned flour.

Preheat the oven to 200°C/400°F/Gas Mark 6. Melt a good piece of the flavoured butter in a large frying pan with an ovenproof handle. When it bubbles up, add the fish. Fry for a couple of minutes, then turn and brown on the other side. Now squeeze a load of lemon juice over.

Move the fish to one side, and add the spuds. Cook for 2 minutes, then add the tomatoes and cook for a further 2 minutes. Finally, add the chokes and season well.

Arrange it all nicely in the pan and pop in the oven for 3–4 minutes to crisp up. Squeeze the rest of the lemon over, sprinkle with lots of parsley, and serve.

Halibut in velvety yogurt sauce with coconut beans

I'm not even sure where I got this recipe, I can't decide if it came from a friend's mum or from a friend who went to India. Anyway, this is a rich, flavoursome sauce that is perfect with the firm texture of halibut. If you fancy something different, then monkfish or any other firm white fish will be good, too.

Serves ④

100ml/3½fl oz vegetable oil

4 x 150g/5oz halibut fillets

seasoned plain flour for dusting

2 large onions, finely chopped

2.5cm/1in piece ginger, grated

pinch each turmeric, cinnamon and ground cloves

175g/6oz natural yogurt

1 tbsp fresh coriander

salt

Coconut beans

500g/1lb green beans

35ml/1½fl oz vegetable oil

½ tsp mustard seeds

pinch turmeric

2 small green chillies, deseeded and chopped

100g/3½oz creamed coconut, taken from a block

Heat a little of the oil in a frying pan, dust the fish in seasoned flour and fry for 1 minute on each side. Take out of the pan, add the rest of the oil and fry the onions gently for 15 minutes until golden.

Add the ginger, turmeric, cinnamon, cloves and salt, stir well, then add the yogurt and coriander. Blend the mix until smooth and return to the pan. When it is hot, pop the fish back in for 2 minutes.

Meanwhile, make the beans: blanch them for 1 minute and refresh. Heat the oil, and when hot but not smoking, add the seeds. After they've popped, add the turmeric and chillies and stir-fry for a minute. Grate the coconut on top.

Serve the beans with the fish and sauce.

Rendang monkfish curry

A proper rendang uses buffalo or bison, cooked really slowly until all the sauce has been absorbed to make a dryish curry with the meat falling apart and tender. The thing is, I love the taste of the sauce, it is delicious as a wetter sauce and it works really well with a fleshy, flavoursome fish like monkfish. Try it yourself.

Serves ④

4 x 150g/5oz monkfish fillets, cut into large chunks

juice 2 limes

pinch each salt and sugar

oil for frying

200g/7oz block creamed coconut

50g/2oz dessicated coconut, toasted

400ml/14fl oz can coconut milk

Rendang curry paste

1 onion, roughly chopped

2 garlic cloves

2.5cm/1in piece of ginger, chopped

3 red chillies, deseeded

1 tsp ground coriander

1 tbsp tamarind paste

1 tsp turmeric

2 tsp curry powder

1 lemon grass stalk

splash oil (optional)

salt

jasmine rice, lime wedges and chopped coriander to serve

Marinate the fish in the lime juice, sugar and salt for at least 30 minutes.

Put all the paste ingredients in a blender with a little salt and mix until smooth. Add a splash of oil if the mixture is a bit dry.

Heat some oil in a wok and fry the paste until fragrant, but be careful not to burn it. Add the creamed coconut a little at a time. Add the fish, toasted coconut and the coconut milk, also a little at a time. Cook over a medium heat until the fish is cooked, about 5 minutes.

Remove the fish, then simmer the sauce to reduce by half. Pop the fish back in to warm through.

Serve with jasmine rice, coriander and lime wedges.

Blackened halibut with mango chutney

This blackening mix brings a bland bit of meat or fish to life, but when you use it with a scrummy piece of halibut like I have here well, it's awesome. Also, you know all those dodgy dried herbs in the cupboard? Why don't you play around with them and make your own blackening compounds.

Serves ④

Mango chutney
olive oil for frying

2.5cm/1in piece of ginger, peeled and minced

1 small red chilli, deseeded

zest and juice of 1 lime

1 garlic clove, crushed

pinch each ground cinnamon and coriander

225g/7½oz soft light brown sugar

225ml/7½fl oz cider vinegar

3 mangoes, peeled and diced

Blackening mix
3 tbsp cayenne

2 tsp mustard powder

2 tsp dried oregano

4 tsp garlic powder

3 tsp onion powder

1 tsp celery salt

pinch thyme

2 tsp white pepper

4 x 150g/5oz halibut steaks

salt and freshly ground black pepper

lime wedges, fresh coriander and rice or chips to serve

First make the chutney. Heat the oil in a large frying pan and gently fry the ginger, chilli, lime zest and juice and garlic until soft. Add the cinnamon, coriander, sugar, vinegar and mango. Bring to the boil, then simmer for at least 40 minutes until it becomes lovely and jammy.

Meanwhile, make the blackening compound by simply mixing all the ingredients together. Then season the fish steaks and press them into the mix, on both sides, and shake off any excess.

Dry-fry in a hot pan for about 2–3 minutes on each side until just cooked. Serve with lime wedges and fresh coriander and rice or chips.

Sole fillets with asparagus

This lovely, flavoursome dish is a good, tasty starter with lots of layers of flavour. A quick tip: oil the steamer to prevent the fish from sticking and always make sure that the water is really on a rolling boil before putting the sole in to steam.

Serves ④

Pesto
handful basil

1 tsp pine nuts

1 garlic clove, crushed

100g/3½oz Parmesan cheese

salt and freshly ground black pepper

100ml/3½fl oz extra virgin olive oil

1 carrot, finely sliced

1 red pepper, finely sliced

4 asparagus spears, finely sliced

2 sole fillets, cut in half lengthways

juice ½ lemon

100ml/3½fl oz double cream

12 sun-blush tomatoes, chopped

Make the pesto by blitzing all the ingredients together, except the oil. When combined, keep the motor running and add the oil. Adjust the seasoning as necessary.

Blanch the carrot, pepper and asparagus and drain well. Lay the sole fillets on a board and season well. Place some of the vegetable mix on one end of each fillet, roll up, and secure with cocktail sticks. Squeeze over some lemon juice, and steam for 4–6 minutes.

To serve, heat some pesto, together with the cream and sun-blush tomatoes, place on a plate and top with one fillet of the fish per person.

Confit salmon

Now, I'm sure like me you all love confit duck – you know, slow cooked in fat, so it makes the duck leg meat really tender. Well, guess what? You can do it with fish, too. Salmon is brilliant for this as it has a high fat content already. I'm doing it in olive oil, but feel free to use duck fat. I would have told you how this dish turns out, but that would spoil the fantastic taste surprise at the end.

Serves 4

1 cucumber, peeled, deseeded and sliced into half moons

1 tbsp mirin (sweetened rice wine)

1 tsp sugar

pinch cayenne

5 tsp soured cream

50g/2oz creamed horseradish

500ml/17fl oz extra virgin olive oil

4 x 125g/4oz salmon fillets

pinch roasted szechuan peppercorns

1 tsp sugar

chopped dill

zest 1 lime

sea salt

watercress, oil and vinegar to serve

First, salt the cucumber for 30 minutes, then rinse and pat dry. Put in a bowl and add the mirin and a pinch of sugar. Chill for 1 hour. Whisk together the cayenne, sour cream and horseradish, then mix with the chilled cucumber.

Meanwhile, gently warm the oil and drop in the salmon, the peppercorns, the sugar, the dill and lime zest. Cook very slowly for about 15 minutes.

To serve, remove the salmon from the oil, draining well, and place it on top of the cucumber. Toss the watercress in a little oil and vinegar and place on the side of the plate.

Soused mackerel

Pickling anything, myself included, is brilliant: it changes all the flavours, and often the texture, of the raw ingredient. We always associate mackerel with strong, sometimes over-powering flavours. Well, souse it and be amazed at how it softens the taste.

Serves ④

1 red pepper

450ml/¾ pint red wine vinegar

50g/2oz sugar

juice 1 lemon

handful thyme

1 tbsp dried chilli flakes

10 saffron threads

625g/1¼lb fresh mackerel fillets, cut into 5cm/2in diamonds

50ml/2fl oz olive oil

4 garlic cloves, sliced

1 tsp mustard seeds

salt and freshly ground black pepper

Grill or roast the red pepper for 10 minutes in a hot oven so you can peel it, then peel, deseed and dice it.

In a pan put the vinegar, sugar, lemon juice, thyme, chilli flakes, saffron and seasoning. Bring to a simmer, then add the fish (adding a little water if needed to cover the fish). Simmer for 5 minutes. Remove from the heat and allow to cool.

Meanwhile, heat the oil and sauté the diced pepper until soft. Add the garlic and mustard seeds and cook for 3–4 minutes.

Place the mackerel on individual plates, stacked up if you wish, and spoon over the liquid, then garnish with the peppers.

Roast hake with gazpacho

I love eating a meal that makes you feel really great afterwards, and this is such a dish. It's full of lovely fresh tastes that blend so well together. All it needs with it is a chunk of crusty bread and a glass of Rueda Blanco for sheer perfection.

Serves ④

2 cucumbers

150ml/¼ pint extra virgin olive oil

50ml/2fl oz sherry vinegar

1 red chilli, deseeded and chopped

plain flour for dusting

4 x 150g/5oz hake fillets with skin on

butter for brushing

400g/13oz cherry tomatoes, on the vine, preferably both red and yellow

good pinch chilli flakes

salt and freshly ground black pepper

First, make the gazpacho. Cut a 7cm/3in piece of cucumber. Deseed, dice finely and set aside. Peel and deseed the remaining cucumber and pulse in a blender until broken down but still with a little chunkiness. Mix all the cucumber together in a bowl and stir in 100ml/3½fl oz of the oil, the vinegar and the chilli and season. There is no need to chill it as you would a traditional gazpacho.

Preheat the oven to 200°C/400°F/Gas Mark 6. Dust a little flour on the skin of the hake, then brush with butter. Season, then cook skin-side down in a hot oiled pan for 3 minutes. Flip over and then roast for 6–8 minutes in the oven, together with seasoned cherry tomatoes and the remaining olive oil.

To serve, place some gazpacho, at room-temperature or even warmed a little if you wish, in a bowl, then place a hake fillet on top and scatter with the chilli flakes. Place some tomatoes at the side.

Merluza a la vasca (Basque hake)

I absolutely adore Spanish food. The tastes are always big and robust and there is such huge diversity in influences. This lovely dish would traditionally not have the sauce reduced and thickened, but I think it makes it even better because of the richness the butter gives it.

Serves ⑥

875g/1¾lb hake, cut into big pieces

plain flour for dredging, seasoned with salt and paprika

olive oil for frying

1 onion, chopped

6 garlic cloves, chopped

225ml/7½fl oz fresh fish stock

225ml/7½fl oz white wine

12 asparagus spears, trimmed

12 small clams, scrubbed

12 mussels, scrubbed and beards removed

100g/3½oz peas

4 eggs, hard-boiled

juice 1 lemon

50g/2oz melted butter

chopped parsley and lemon wedges to garnish

Preheat the oven to 180°C/350°F/Gas Mark 4. Dredge the fish in flour. Heat the oil in a frying pan and fry the fish for 1 minute on each side. Place in a single layer in an ovenproof dish. Fry the onion and garlic in the same pan then layer them on top of the fish.

Place the stock and wine in the frying pan, then deglaze the pan, scraping off all the lovely bits at the bottom. Bring the liquid to a boil, let it reduce by one-third, then pour it over the fish. Lay the asparagus on top. Press the clams and mussels into the gaps, cover and bake for 8 minutes. Add the peas and egg and return to the oven for a few minutes more.

Divide the fish mixture between 6 plates and sprinkle over the lemon juice and the melted butter.

Serve, garnished with parsley and lemon wedges.

Cod in coconut milk with spiced mussels

Quite simply, this is a delicious fish supper – creamy, flavourful and the mussels around it give it a bit of extra taste and texture. It also works rather well if you grill or fry the fish after you have marinated it.

Serves ④

400ml/14fl oz can coconut milk

juice 1 lemon

35ml/1½fl oz olive oil

4 x 150g/5oz cod steaks

50g/2oz butter

200g/7oz breadcrumbs

25g/1oz coriander, finely chopped

1 garlic clove, crushed

1 red chilli, deseeded and finely chopped

12 green lip mussels, cooked and in their shells

salt and freshly ground black pepper

rice to serve

Mix the coconut milk, lemon juice, oil and seasoning together in a dish. Marinate the fish for at least 1 hour, covered, in the fridge. Just before you are ready to cook, preheat the oven to 180°C/350°F/Gas Mark 4. Drain the fish, place in a roasting tin and roast for 4–6 minutes.

Meanwhile, bring the drained marinade to the boil and reduce by half.

Make a topping for the mussels by combining the butter, crumbs, coriander, garlic and chilli in a bowl. Press on to the mussels, then grill for a couple of minutes to crisp.

Arrange the mussels around the cod on each plate and drizzle the sauce over the top. Serve with rice.

Salmon, fennel and peanut salad

Happy accident time. This recipe came about when I was playing with dressings … Mmmm, what would be nice with fennel? I could poach that bit of salmon in the refrigerator. 'Voilà': a+b=c.

Serves ⑥–⑧

2 tbsp salt

1 tsp white peppercorns

2 bay leaves

1 fennel bulb, including top

4 x 175g/6oz salmon fillets

300g/10oz fine beans, cooked

200g/7oz sugarsnap peas, cooked

Dressing

3 plum tomatoes

2 anchovy fillets (can be either salted or fresh)

1 onion, finely diced

juice 2 limes

50ml/2fl oz groundnut oil

basil leaves, torn

1 red chilli, deseeded and finely chopped

splash Thai fish sauce

30g/1½oz roasted peanuts, crushed

Put the salt and peppercorns, bay leaves and fennel top in a pan with about 600ml/1 pint water. Bring to the boil and then take off the heat. Put the salmon in, cover and leave for 15 minutes, then remove the salmon and allow to cool.

To make the dressing, simply combine all the ingredients in a blender, then pulse until smoothish, yet chunky.

Blanch the fennel bulb, then finely slice it. Break the salmon into large chunks, then toss these with the beans and sugarsnaps and season. Finally, pour over the dressing.

Veg

Braised fennel with orange and anchovy

Mostly, I like my veggies to be al dente, but there are times when soft, succulent vegetables work so much better, allowing all the flavour to develop. This is such a dish. Serve as a really funky side dish.

Serves ⑥

300g/10oz fennel

125ml/4fl oz olive oil for frying

pinch dried chilli flakes

1 garlic clove, crushed

4 salted anchovies

25ml/1fl oz maple syrup

zest 1 orange

salt and freshly ground black pepper

Cut the fennel into quarters, if medium to large, or halves if small. Place in a saucepan of boiling salted water and cook until soft, about 8 minutes. Drain.

Take a frying pan big enough to hold all the fennel, laid side by side. In it, heat the oil until hot, then pop in the chilli flakes, garlic and anchovies and stir fry until the anchovies are dissolving. Now add the maple syrup and stir well. Next add the fennel and coat well with the sauce.

Cook for about 5 minutes, then stir in the zest at the last minute and serve.

Feta, courgette and spinach tart

I imagine it to be summertime when I'm eating this, so if it's winter and you fancy a bit of escapism, make this, turn the heating up full, pop on the summer gear and make all your family pretend they're in Greece with you … because you're worth it.

Serves at least (6)

Pastry case
225g/7½oz plain flour
100g/3½oz butter
50ml/2fl oz milk
salt

Filling
400g/13oz spinach
3 eggs
400ml/14fl oz double cream
2 garlic cloves, crushed
a little grated nutmeg
50g/2oz toasted pine nuts
200g/7oz feta cheese, diced small
butter for frying
4–6 courgettes, sliced
2 tbsp grated Parmesan cheese
a few cherry tomatoes, halved
oil for drizzling
salt and freshly ground black pepper

dressed rocket to serve

First make the pastry. Pulse the flour and butter in a blender until it looks like damp crumbs. Now turn it out into a bowl, add the milk and seasoning and form into a dough. Cover and chill for 20 minutes. Roll out to easily fill a 20cm/8in tart case, and chill again for at least 1 hour.

Preheat the oven to 200°C/400°F/Gas Mark 6. Trim back any extra pastry, prick the base with a fork, line with foil and sit either baking beads or raw rice on top, then bake for 20 minutes until cooked, taking the foil off once the sides are cooked. Remove from the oven and turn the heat down to 180°C/350°F/Gas Mark 4.

Meanwhile, prepare the filling. Cook the spinach in a little water, for about 4–5 minutes, then press out all the moisture and season well. In a large bowl, beat together the eggs, cream, half the garlic, salt and pepper and nutmeg, then add the spinach, pine nuts and half the feta.

Melt the butter in a frying pan, add the courgette and remaining garlic and fry until soft, then drain on kitchen paper. Add to the egg mix then spoon into the baked pastry case and top with the Parmesan.

Top with the tomatoes and the rest of the feta. Drizzle over a little oil and bake for 45 minutes. Serve a good wedge at room temperature with dressed rocket.

Veggie black pudding and lavender salad

It's rare that I get so excited by a new product: the cynical old chef that I am, I think I've seen it all. But Ireland Black Puddings does a fantastic veggie black pud, which is a real winner. In this recipe, I've matched it with a creamy lavender dressing. It seems to complement it perfectly. Serve it as a starter.

Serves ④ (dressing serves 8)

oil for frying and roasting

16 small potatoes, cooked

12 slices of vegetarian black pudding (cut about 1.5cm/¾in thick)

good handful rocket

12 asparagus spears, blanched

salt and freshly ground black pepper

Dressing

4 egg yolks

4 tsp sugar

4 tsp Dijon mustard

600ml/1 pint olive oil

200ml/7fl oz white wine vinegar

juice 3 lemons

1 tbsp dried lavender, very finely chopped, plus extra for garnishing

salt and freshly ground black pepper

Preheat the oven to 220°C/425°F/Gas Mark 7. Put a good quantity of olive oil in an ovenproof dish and pop it into the very hot oven, until smoking. Now put in the spuds, season well, shake carefully and roast for about 30 minutes until crisp, giving them a little turn every now and again

Cover the bottom of a frying pan with more oil and heat until hot, but not smoking. Place the pudding slices in, and cook for about 1 minute on each side, until just crisp. Drain on kitchen paper.

To make the dressing, beat the egg yolks in a blender. Add the sugar, seasoning and mustard and combine. With the blender on, slowly add the oil, and with the motor still running slowly, add the vinegar. Finally, add the lemon juice and then the chopped lavender.

To assemble the salad, put the spuds and rocket in a bowl with a good spoonful or two of the dressing and toss together. Divide this between 4 plates, then sit 3 pieces of pudding tightly around the spuds and arrange the asparagus on top. Spoon over a little more dressing, add a twist of black pepper and some extra crushed lavender to garnish.

Beer soup

Yeah, I know, sounds weird doesn't it? So simple and so delicious. You can use this recipe as a starting point for slightly different flavours, with different types of beer: noone will believe it's beer. Trust me!

Serves ⑥

30g/1½oz butter for frying

1 large onion, sliced

300ml/½ pint stout or bitter

300ml/½ pint vegetable stock

2 large potatoes, cut into large cubes

2 tsp sugar

salt and freshly ground black pepper

In a large saucepan melt the butter and fry the onions gently and slowly until caramelized, about 20 minutes. Add the beer, stock, spuds and sugar, then cook for 30 minutes more.

Finally, purée until smooth, season and serve.

Indian parcels

I put this dish on the menu at Greens about 6 months ago and it just flies out of the kitchen. Which is not surprising since it has everything a good dish needs: texture, taste, colour. It's impossible not to want more, especially with this rich, medium-heat bhuna curry sauce. Even when you're full to bursting.

Serves (6)

1 packet ready-rolled pastry

Filling

1 tsp each of cumin seeds and coriander seeds

400g/13oz sweet potatoes, cubed and blanched

200g/7oz asparagus, blanched and roughly chopped

400g/13oz can chickpeas, well rinsed and drained

1 tbsp curry leaves

2 small green chillies deseeded and chopped

1 tbsp roughly chopped fresh coriander

salt and freshly ground black pepper

Bhuna

oil for frying

2 tsp each of mustard seeds and cumin seeds

1 onion, sliced

2.5cm/1in piece of ginger, peeled and cut into matchsticks

1 garlic clove, crushed

1 tsp turmeric

1 heaped tbsp curry powder

625g/1¼lb cherry tomatoes

salt and freshly ground black pepper

1 egg, beaten to glaze and sesame seeds to sprinkle on top

coriander leaves and yogurt to serve

Roll out the pastry and cut into 6 x 20cm/8in squares.

Next, prepare the filling. Dry fry the spices, then toss together the sweet spuds, asparagus, chickpeas, curry leaves, chillies, coriander and plenty of seasoning. Divide the mix between the 6 pieces of pastry and roll up into very tight balls; keep them really tight and they'll look so much better.

Now brush with eggwash, top with a sprinkle of sesame seeds and chill for 20 minutes. Preheat the oven to 200°C/400°F/Gas Mark 6 and after chilling the parcels, place them on a baking tray and cook them in the oven for 25 minutes until crisp and golden.

Meanwhile, make the bhuna, heat the oil in a frying pan until hot, chuck in the mustard and cumin seeds until they pop (only a matter of seconds), then fry the onion and ginger until the onion is a golden colour. This will take a good 20 minutes and you'll need to stir it pretty regularly.

Now add the garlic, turmeric and curry powder, stir well then add the tomatoes. Cook really slowly until the tomatoes start to break down, about 20 minutes, and check the seasoning.

Serve a parcel with a spoonful of bhuna at the side, a sprinkling of coriander and a good dollop of yogurt.

Tagliatelle with beetroot

Any dish that looks like Barbie made it and tastes as fantastic as this has to be tried. What you'll get is a spicy, vibrant and yes, pink but scrummy pasta, with a wicked kick. Bring it on!

Serves ④

8 fresh beetroot
1 cinnamon stick
2 shallots
1 garlic clove, crushed
125ml/4fl oz white wine
225ml/7½fl oz chicken stock
250ml/8fl oz soured cream
1 tbsp fresh dill
1 tbsp horseradish cream
400g/13oz cooked fresh tagliatelle
salt and freshly ground black pepper

Parmesan shavings to serve

Preheat the oven to 200°C/400°F/Gas Mark 6. Wipe the beets clean, season, then wrap them in foil with the cinnamon stick and roast for 45 minutes until soft. Cool, unwrap and peel, then chop them up nice and fine.

Fry the shallot and garlic until soft, add the wine, bring to the boil and reduce by two-thirds. Add the stock, return to the boil, then reduce by about half. Add the beets and soured cream, return to the boil and reduce to a thick sauce.

Fold in the dill and horseradish, spoon over the pasta and serve with Parmesan shavings.

Yogurt tahini sauce

Sauce, dip, call it what you fancy, this is a really lovely combination. The tahini slightly dries the yogurt and gives it a bit more oomph. Great with lamb (chops, kebabs), spinach and, in fact, most Middle Eastern and Mediterranean dishes.

Makes 250g/8oz

2 garlic cloves
2.5cm/1in piece of ginger, sliced
1 tbsp fresh coriander, leaves and stalk
200g/7oz natural yogurt
65g/2½oz tahini paste
juice 1 lemon
dash sesame oil
salt and freshly ground black pepper

Put the garlic, ginger and coriander in a blender and blitz together. Now simply mix all the remaining ingredients together, combine with the blitzed mixture and season. Easy!

Peas and lettuce

A massive bowlful of this delicious combination is perfect served with roast chicken, pork chops or sausages.

Serves ④

50ml/2fl oz olive oil
50g/2oz butter
200g/7oz pearl onions (use canned or frozen if necessary, but not pickled)
1 tbsp thyme
1 bay leaf
125ml/4fl oz vegetable stock
500g/1lb peas (fresh or frozen)
2 baby gem lettuce, roughly chopped
salt and freshly ground black pepper

Heat the oil and butter in a large frying pan, and when it begins to bubble fry the onions, thyme and bay leaf for about 5 minutes. Now add the stock and peas and simmer for 12 minutes.

Stir in the lettuce just before serving, and season.

① ② ④ Veg

Jersey Royals, watercress and radish salad

If ever there was proof that a good simple recipe needs smashing ingredients, then this is it. I can never get enough Jersey Royals, but I am glad that the season is short because it keeps them special. If you can't get them, or the season's over then something like a lovely small Anya is nearly as good.

Serves (6)

Dressing
(makes about 1 litre/1¾ pints)

5 egg yolks

4 tbsp caster sugar

4 tbsp Dijon mustard

600ml/1 pint extra virgin olive oil

150ml/¼ pint white wine vinegar

juice 3 large lemons

good handful chopped fresh oregano

salt and freshly ground black pepper

750g/1½lb Jersey Royals, cooked and cooled

250g/8oz radishes, cut into thick rounds

2 banana shallots, halved lengthways and cut into very fine half moons

2 good bunches watercress

crusty French bread to serve

First make the dressing. Pop the yolks in a blender and blitz smooth. Now add the sugar and mustard and blitz again. Leave the motor running and slowly add the oil. When it's all combined, do the same with the vinegar. Finally, add the lemon juice and fold in the oregano and seasoning.

For the salad, well it couldn't be simpler. Pop the spuds in a large bowl – they should be the size of a good mouthful, so cut down any that are too big. Add the radishes (I chuck away the top and bottom of these – chuck into my mouth that is) and the shallots. Season well and spoon over a generous amount of the dressing.

Trim off the bottom of the watercress and gently toss it in with the other ingredients (spreading your fingers wide, so as not to damage the watercress) and add a good twist of black pepper.

I serve the salad in a huge bowl, let everyone dig in and have a jug of extra dressing and crusty French bread for everyone to share.

Unbelievable onion rings

My daughter, Flo, discovered the joys of onion rings on a trip to Spain. Now don't get me wrong, I love the shop-bought, addictive ones, but these fat, juicy, buttermilk-soaked boys are the greatest addition to a pint since they started showing football matches in pubs.

Serves ⑥

1 large sweet white onion
1 litre/1¾ pints buttermilk
175g/6oz plain flour
50g/2oz polenta
1½ tbsp sea salt
freshly ground black pepper
1 tbsp chilli powder
oil for deep-frying

balsamic vinegar to serve

Slice the onion into 1cm/½in thick rings. Soak the separated rings in the buttermilk for about 30 minutes. Give them the odd stir.

Sift together the flour, polenta, salt, pepper and chilli on to a plate. Heat the oil in a deep-frier or wok to about 180°C/350°F. Take one ring at a time from the buttermilk and make sure there's lots of buttermilk clinging to the onion. Coat batches of about 6 in the flour mix, and don't shake off the excess. Deep-fry these for about 3–4 minutes until crisp and golden. They will probably sink to the bottom at first, but will swim majestically to the top as they cook; keep them moving. Drain on kitchen paper, and repeat until they're all done.

Serve immediately, with a sprinkling of salt, and a little balsamic vinegar to dip into.

Simple green salad, Chinese style

What is this doing in a recipe book? I hear you ask. Well, the dressing and seasoning are the stars here and need no more than a few crunchy bits of greenery to make it a firm favourite.

Serves ④

½ iceberg lettuce, roughly chopped

1 bunch fresh mint

1 tbsp coriander leaves

100g/3½oz baby red chard

1 tbsp Szechuan peppercorns

1 tbsp coarse sea salt

Dressing

100ml/3½fl oz extra virgin olive oil

50ml/2fl oz dark malt vinegar

25ml/1fl oz light soy sauce

1 garlic clove, crushed

1 tsp suagr

Pop the iceberg into a large bowl with all the other leaves.

Gently dry-fry the peppercorns in a frying pan for 4–5 minutes until fragrant, taking care not to burn them. Then crush them in a mortar and pestle until pretty smooth.

For the dressing, just whisk all the ingredients together in a bowl. To serve, gently toss the leaves in the dressing and sprinkle over the peppercorn mix.

Yorkshire puddings with red-onion gravy

More food to watch football and drink beer with. Do feel free to add rare roast beef to this one.

Serves ④–⑥

Yorkshire pudding batter

150g/5oz plain flour

1 tsp salt

2 eggs

150ml/¼ pint milk

2 tbsp vegetable oil

4 tbsp cold water

Red onion gravy

2 tbsp olive oil

2 red onions, sliced

50g/2oz mushrooms, roughly chopped

2 tsp fresh thyme

2 tbsp plain flour

125ml/4fl oz red wine

1 tsp balsamic vinegar

250ml/8fl oz vegetable stock

1 tbsp soy sauce

For the batter, sift the flour and salt into a bowl. In a jug, beat the eggs with the milk. Make a well in the centre of the flour and gradually beat in the milk mixture. Keep stirring until you have a smooth, thick batter. You may need to add a little more milk if the batter is very thick. Leave to stand for 1 hour.

To make the gravy, heat the oil in a pan, add the onions and cook slowly over a low to medium heat until they begin to caramelize and turn golden (30–40 minutes). Meanwhile, preheat the oven to 220°C/425°F/Gas Mark 7. Pour the vegetable oil into a large ovenproof dish or Yorkshire pudding tin. Place in the hot oven until smoking hot. After resting, the batter will have thickened. Add the cold water and give one last beat.

Remove the Yorkshire pudding tin from the oven. Pour the batter on to the sizzling oil so it comes half way up the tin. Return to the oven and bake for 15 minutes. Lower the heat to 200°C/400°F/Gas Mark 6 and cook for 15 minutes more, or until the puddings are crisp and well risen. Remove and keep warm.

To finish the gravy, add the mushrooms and thyme to the onions and cook for 5 minutes. Sprinkle in the flour and stir for 2 minutes. Pour in the wine and keep stirring. Add the vinegar, the stock and soy sauce and simmer for 3–5 minutes until the gravy thickens slightly. Pour over the Yorkshire puddings and serve.

Stuffed aubergine rolls

Never trust anyone who doesn't like aubergines! How can you not like the juicy, meaty, smoky flavour of these purple gods? This dish is so simple and makes a scrummy starter. A word of advice: they taste better for being a little overcooked rather than under.

Serves (4)

2 aubergines, cut lengthways into 2.5mm/⅛in thick strips

olive oil for brushing

salt and freshly ground black pepper

Filling

150g/5oz ricotta

150g/5oz buffalo mozzarella

pinch freshly grated nutmeg

2 spring onions, finely chopped

Sauce

250ml/8fl oz extra virgin olive oil

500g/1lb cherry tomatoes, halved

1 garlic clove, crushed

pinch sugar

salt and freshly ground black pepper

Season the aubergine slices well and brush with the oil. Griddle for a couple of minutes on each side in a hot griddle pan and drain on kitchen paper.

Mix together the cheeses, nutmeg and onion in a bowl. Lay out all the slices of aubergine and place about one tablespoon of filling at the bottom edge of each one. Roll up nice and tightly and rest them seam-side down on a plate.

Next, make the sauce. Heat the oil and drop in all the halved cherry tomatoes. Now simmer for about 8 minutes until the tomatoes begin to break down. Take off the heat, stir in the garlic and sugar and add some salt and pepper.

Preheat the oven to 180°C/350°F/Gas Mark 4. Spoon some of the sauce on to the bottom of an ovenproof dish. Sit the aubergine rolls on top, and spoon over the rest of the sauce. Bake for about 15 minutes until the cheese begins to melt – heaven.

Deep-fried cauliflower in choux pastry

You know how sometimes when you make fritters and the like, by the time you get them to the table they've gone all soggy? Well, using a choux-pastry-type batter keeps 'em really crispy. Blitz some fresh mint leaves with yogurt to make a dip and away you go.

Makes about ②⓪

225ml/7½fl oz water
225g/7½oz butter
pinch salt
150g/5oz plain flour
1 red chilli, deseeded and finely chopped
pinch turmeric
6 eggs
oil to deep-fry
1 head cauliflower, cut into florets

300ml/½ pint plain yoghurt and 1 tbsp finely chopped mint to serve

Bring the water, butter and salt to the boil, then take off the heat and tip in all the flour, the chilli and the turmeric. Mix well, then return to a low heat and keep beating until the dough comes away from the side of the pan. Take off the heat, then beat in the eggs, one at a time.

Bring the oil up to 180°C/350°F in a deep-fat frier or wok. Meanwhile, blanch the cauli for 2 minutes. Dip the florets in the batter and coat well – I like to use two spoons to lift them as this keeps the batter in better shape.

Now, in small batches, deep-fry the florets until they're golden brown and drain on kitchen paper.

Mix the yoghurt through with the chopped mint, and serve it as a dip to go with the cauliflower, or serve the cauliflower on its own as a crazy alternative vegetable.

Fennel with champagne, honey and polenta

Too big to be a starter, so lunch, brunch or a snack, that's what this is. I love the combination of creamy polenta and the aniseed of the fennel. The ideal companion for this is, obviously, a glass of bubbly.

Serves ⑥

6 fennel bulbs

juice 2 lemons

50g/2oz butter

4 tsp honey

200ml/7fl oz champagne or sparkling wine

750ml/1¼ pints milk

2 garlic cloves, chopped

175g/6oz instant polenta

125g/4oz Parmesan cheese, grated

extra virgin olive oil for frying and drizzling

4 shallots, finely chopped

300g/10oz baby spinach

100g/3½oz rocket

salt and freshly ground black pepper

Parmesan shavings to serve

Trim the fennel, and cut into quarters. Cover with the lemon juice, salt and pepper and just enough water to cover. Bring to the boil and simmer for 10 minutes, then drain.

Put the butter and honey in a pan and heat until it bubbles. Throw in the fennel and cook until it browns slightly. Add the booze and reduce to a syrup. Take off the heat

For the polenta, bring the milk and garlic to the boil, then add the polenta in a smooth stream, to avoid lumps. Keep stirring for 4–6 minutes, then season and add the cheese.

Heat some oil in a large saucepan and cook the shallots until softened, then add the greens, season and wilt for a couple of minutes.

To serve, spoon some of the creamy, cheesy polenta into the middle of a plate, drizzle with olive oil, sit some greens on top, then the fennel, then the syrupy sauce and a few Parmesan shavings – scrummy!

Herby risotto with fennel and creamed tomato

At the back end of summer this is a delicious meal that uses some of the late-summer harvest. The flavours are nice and big, so it also reminds you that the nights are drawing in and you'd best get the central heating serviced.

Serves (4)

2 fennel bulbs, quartered

1 lemon

75ml/3fl oz olive oil

3 garlic cloves, 1 crushed and 2 chopped

450ml/¾ pint double cream

6 plum tomatoes, cut in half lengthways

12 sage leaves

Risotto

2 shallots, finely chopped

450g/14½oz arborio rice

1 tbsp fresh thyme

splash white wine

650ml/1 pint 22fl oz hot vegetable stock

100ml/3½fl oz extra virgin olive oil

salt and freshly ground black pepper

Preheat the oven to 180°C/350°F/Gas Mark 4. Lay the fennel in an ovenproof pan, season, squeeze over the lemon (add the lemon halves to the pan), drizzle with olive oil and sprinkle with the crushed garlic. Roast for 25–30 minutes until soft. Cool a little, remove from the pan and slice into thin strips. Leave the oven on.

Meanwhile, bring the cream to the boil in a heavy-bottomed pan with the chopped garlic and reduce by one-third. Place the tomatoes, cut-side up in an ovenproof pan, season, top with the sage leaves and pour over the reduced cream. Bake for 25 minutes in the still-hot oven.

To make the risotto, fry the shallots until soft. Now add the rice, thyme and wine and stir well. When the husk of the rice begins to crack, add a good ladleful of stock. When all this has been absorbed, add more stock. Continue until the rice is cooked. Season then stir in the fennel and extra virgin olive oil.

Serve a good portion of the risotto, topped with 3 slices of tomato and some of the reduced cream.

Cucumber, mint and fennel chilled soup

Funny things, chilled soups. Aside from gazpacho, there aren't many I like. Having said that, this is a really delicious, light starter at any time of the year. Now you may think it strange to have something like brandy and raisins on top, but they give both a boozy kick and a bit of depth to the soup.

Serves ⑥–⑧

1 cucumber, seeds scooped out and flesh sliced finely

2 garlic cloves, crushed

1 tbsp tarragon vinegar

1 tbsp fresh mint

300ml/½ pint single cream

300ml/½ pint fromage frais

2 eggs, hard-boiled and finely chopped

½ fennel bulb, finely sliced on a mandolin

100g/3½oz raisins, soaked in brandy

salt and freshly ground black pepper

Either mix all the ingredients bar the raisins together coarsely or blitz until really smooth, it's up to you. Personally, I prefer it smooth. Chill thoroughly.

Serve really well chilled in shot glasses or espresso cups, with a few room-temperature boozy raisins on top of each.

Mushroom and Parmesan torte

This is a firm favourite at our house, one of those lunch, tea, supper and cold-for-breakfast dishes that works well when you're balancing family, restaurant, telly and that lack of a secret eighth day that nobody else knows about.

Serves (8)

75g/3oz butter, plus extra for greasing

175g/6oz Parmesan cheese, finely grated

oil for frying

700g/1lb 6oz button and/or field mushrooms, chopped

2 red onions, finely chopped

225ml/7½fl oz double cream

3 eggs

100g/3½oz frozen peas

Chutney

4 onions, finely chopped

oil for frying

75ml/3fl oz vinegar

1 garlic clove, crushed

1 tbsp chilli paste or sauce

75g/3oz brown sugar

salt and freshly ground black pepper

dressed leaves to serve

Grease a 20cm/8oz springform tin and dust with a little of the Parmesan. Heat the oil and butter in a frying pan and fry the mushrooms until soft with the onions and salt and pepper. Cool, then purée half of them to a paste. Combine this paste with the rest of the mushroom mixture, the cream, eggs, peas and half of the remaining cheese.

Preheat the oven to 200°C/400°F/Gas Mark 6. Spoon the mixture into the tin, top with the rest of the Parmesan and then bake for 45–50 minutes until set. Allow to cool, then turn out.

Meanwhile, make the chutney by frying the onions in oil until soft, then add the vinegar, garlic, chilli and sugar. Cook long and low for 45 minutes, stirring occasionally.

Serve a spoonful of the chutney with a big wedge of torte and some dressed leaves.

Potato in yogurt

This is one of my secret weapons: so simple but so special that I almost didn't share it with you. Serve this flavoursome side dish with, well, just about anything to be honest.

Serves (6)

1 tsp cumin seeds

300ml/½ pint natural yogurt

300ml/½ pint water

pinch turmeric

1 tsp chilli powder

1 tsp ground coriander

1 tsp cumin

1 tsp dark brown sugar

25ml 1oz vegetable oil

handful fresh coriander

2 green chillies, deseeded and chopped

450g/14½oz potatoes, cubed and par-boiled

salt

Gently fry the cumin seeds for 3 minutes in a dry pan, to release the oils.

Combine the yogurt, water, turmeric, chilli powder, ground coriander, cumin, salt and sugar and add this mixture to the pan. Add the oil and cook for 3 minutes.

Add the fresh coriander, chillies and spuds and simmer for 8 minutes. Scrummy!

Aubergine, mint and balsamic salad

Just the thought of this salad makes me salivate, it is sooo delicious. It's also one of those lovely recipes that works in all seasons, and is great as a starter.

Serves ⑥

3 aubergines, cut into 2.5mm/⅛in thick rounds

75ml/3fl oz olive oil, plus extra for brushing

3 onions, finely sliced

2 x 400g/13oz cans plum tomatoes

pinch sugar

5 tbsp good-quality balsamic vinegar

large handful mint

salt and freshly ground black pepper

about 12 fresh marinated anchovies and chunky bread to serve

Brush the aubergine slices with a little oil, season well and griddle for 1 minute on each side, until they're nice and charred. Lay out on kitchen paper in a single layer to cool.

Heat the olive oil in a frying pan and fry the onion until softening and just beginning to colour, probably about 3–4 minutes. Drain the tomatoes and add them to the pan, turn up the heat and cook for a minute, stirring all the time. Add the sugar and season well.

Now put the aubergines in a large bowl, cover with the tomato mix, add the vinegar and mint. Now toss very gently, to keep the aubergines whole. Let it cool to just about room temperature.

Top with chopped, fresh anchovies to serve and have some chunky bread to dip in.

Goats' cheese cake with cider and apple chutney

This works well as either a starter or an alternative cheese course, as it is a bit sweet and savoury at the same time. If you happen to have individual little cake tins, then use them to make very personal cheesecakes.

Serves ⑧

Base
300g/10oz oat cakes crushed
150g/5oz butter, melted
200g/7oz fig jam

Topping
800g/1lb 10oz ricotta cheese
200g/7oz goats' cheese
6 eggs
salt and freshly ground black pepper

Chutney
450ml/¾ pint cider
1 onion, finely sliced
1 red chilli, deseeded and chopped
3 apples, chopped
100ml/3½fl oz cider vinegar
100g/3½oz sugar
salt and freshly ground black pepper

rocket to serve

To make the base, combine the oat cakes and butter and press into the base of a 20cm/8in tin. Spread the jam over the base, but leave a gap all around the edge.

Preheat the oven to 180°C/350°F/Gas Mark 4. To make the topping, combine the cheeses, eggs, salt and pepper; you can do this by hand, but it is easier in a food processor. Spoon on to the base, and don't worry if the mix looks too runny: the eggs will set it. Cook in the oven for 50 minutes.

Meanwhile, make the chutney. Pour the cider into a saucepan, bring to the boil and reduce to a thick syrup. In a separate pan, fry the onion with the chilli until soft. Add the apples and cook for about 10 minutes until soft. Add the vinegar and sugar and cook on a very low heat for about 40 minutes. Season well.

Let the cake cool before removing it from the tin. Slice into wedges and spoon some reduced cider over.

Serve with the chutney and maybe a few leaves of peppery rocket.

Barbecue sauce from Nag's Head

One of the most beautiful places I've ever been to is Nag's Head in North Carolina. Ali, my wife, and I went there when she was expecting Flo. We stood on the white sandy beach watching dolphins and wishing we owned one of the beach houses there. This zingy barbecue sauce never fails to remind me of that time. It's a thin sauce to be used as a condiment but, boy, is it great with grilled meat.

Makes about 225ml/7½fl oz

175ml/6fl oz cider vinegar
50ml/2fl oz white vinegar
1 tbsp soft light brown sugar
½ tsp dried chilli flakes
salt and freshly ground black pepper

Simply whisk all the ingredients together, making sure the sugar breaks down. Let it sit for at least 1 hour before using.

Braised lettuce

Because little gem lettuce is so versatile, it's brilliant for braising. It works really well as a side dish for any fish, and I love it finely chopped over a simple white-onion risotto.

Serves ⑥

6 heads little gem (cut in half lengthways if they're huge)
4 shallots, finely chopped
1 garlic clove, finely sliced
about 200ml/7fl oz vegetable stock
salt and freshly ground black pepper

Preheat the oven to 200°C/400°F/Gas Mark 6. Blanch the lettuces in a large saucepan of boiling water for 2 minutes, then drain well.

Lay the lettuce in a single layer in an ovenproof dish. Sprinkle the shallots and garlic over and season well. Now pour in enough stock to come about one-third of the way up the lettuce. Cover with foil and cook for about 8 minutes until soft.

Courgette, tomato and Cheddar muffins

Wherever you go in the USA, the breakfast offering is always immense: pancakes, waffles, bagels, sourdough and so it goes on. Even in all that abundance these aren't a traditional American breakfast dish. But believe me, they should be.

Makes (1)(0) muffins

butter for greasing
225g/7½oz self-raising flour
100g/3½oz grated courgette
100g/3½oz mature Cheddar
175ml/6fl oz milk
1 egg
50ml/2fl oz olive oil
10 cherry tomatoes
salt and freshly ground black pepper

crispy grilled bacon and scrambled egg to serve

Preheat the oven to 200°C/400°F/Gas Mark 6 and grease 10 muffin moulds. In a bowl, combine the flour, courgette, seasoning and Cheddar. In a separate bowl mix together the milk, egg and oil, then add this to the dry ingredients and combine.

Half-fill each muffin hole with the mixture. Now, prick each cherry tomato (this stops them popping when they cook), and sit them on top of the mix. Next, spoon the rest of the mixture over to cover the tomatoes. Cook in the oven for about 20 minutes.

Serve warm immediately with brekkie ingredients, or cool, split in half and toast, then serve buttered with bacon and eggs.

Minestrone

I can't get enough of this lovely soup. Warm, comforting, absolutely delicious.

Serves (4)

1 large onion, sliced

150g/5oz streaky bacon, diced

4 celery sticks, chopped

2 carrots, sliced

2 garlic cloves, crushed

olive oil for frying

2 potatoes, diced

1 litre/1¾ pints beef stock

2 tbsp tomato purée

400g/13oz can haricot beans

1 bay leaf

1 tsp chopped thyme

fresh chopped parsley

400g/13oz can chopped tomatoes

100g/3½oz spaghetti, broken

salt and freshly ground black pepper

finely grated Parmesan cheese and crusty white bread to serve

In a large saucepan heat a little oil and cook the onion, bacon, celery, carrot and garlic for 2 minutes. Then add the spuds and the stock and bring up to the boil.

Next stir in the purée. Simmer for 45 minutes, then add the beans, herbs, tomatoes and pasta and cook until the pasta is soft. Season well, especially with pepper. Serve with the cheese and bread.

Stuffed figs

There's a classic Italian dish that uses Gorgonzola and walnuts in the stuffing for figs. This one uses Butler's Blacksticks Blue, a fantastic Lancashire blue cheese (you can use any blue cheese if you want) and pecans, which I think are a little less bitter. Serve the figs with some Parma ham.

Serves ④

12 ripe figs
150g/5oz Blackstick's Blue
50g/2oz chopped pecans
extra virgin olive oil
freshly ground black pepper

Parma ham to serve

Preheat the oven to 200°C/400°F/Gas Mark 6. Cut a 'cross' in the top of each fig and pop on to a baking sheet. Gently open up each fig.

Mix together the cheese and nuts and spoon about 1 tablespoon of the filling into each fig. Bake in the hot oven for about 6–8 mins until the cheese oozes out. Drizzle with olive oil and add a twist of black pepper. Serve with Parma ham.

Savoy cabbage parcels

These parcels are sort of Greek meets Birkenhead, really. If you feel like something different, try them with kale leaves. Don't you think cabbage and kale are among those things that we all had to eat as kids and hated, much like spinach, but now they're brilliant?

Serves 6–8

6–8 Savoy cabbage (or kale) leaves, hard stems removed, and well-blanched in salted water

Filling

150g/5oz butternut squash, cubed

75ml/3fl oz olive oil

100g/3½oz aubergine, cubed

1 garlic clove, crushed

150g/5oz bulgar wheat, cooked

100g/3½oz puy lentils, cooked

2 tbsp chopped mint

100g/3½oz feta cheese, cubed

salt and freshly ground black pepper

Dip

150g/5oz Greek yogurt

50g/2oz cucumber, grated

juice ½ lemon

1 garlic clove, crushed

salt and freshly ground black pepper

Preheat the oven to 180°C/350°F/Gas Mark 4.

Place the squash and the aubergine in a roasting tin, drizzle over the olive oil, add the garlic and seasoning and cook, until soft (about 30 minutes). Transfer to a bowl and combine with the bulgar wheat, lentils, mint and feta.

Place one tablespoon of the mix in the middle of each cabbage leaf and roll up, securing with a cocktail stick if necessary.

Make the dip by simply combining all the ingredients.

Serve the parcels hot or cold. If you want them hot, pop into an ovenproof dish with a tiny splash of water in the bottom and warm at 180°C/350°F/Gas Mark 4 for about 8 minutes.

Leek and potato rosti

I ate rosti on my wedding day, at Betty's Tea Rooms in York, so they are a big fave of mine. I find that making them with raw potato can be a bit hit and miss, as sometimes the starch holds them together, sometimes not. So by parboiling for 7 minutes, there's just enough starch to get them all gloopy (a well-known technical term) and you'll have perfect rosti every time.

Serves ④

2 large baking potatoes
1 leek, finely sliced
1 garlic clove, crushed
olive oil for frying
4 large field mushrooms
100ml/3½fl oz olive oil
1 garlic clove, crushed
1 tsp chopped thyme
150g/5oz raclette cheese
salt and freshly ground black pepper

tomato chutney to serve

Cook the spuds in their jackets in a saucepan of boiling salted water, for exactly 7 minutes, cool a little, then peel. Grate coarsley, then add the leek, garlic and lots of seasoning. Mould into 4 rostis and chill for 20 minutes. Heat the oil in a frying pan then fry the rostis for 4 minutes on each side until crisp and golden. Drain on kitchen paper.

Preheat the oven to 200°C/400°F/Gas Mark 6. Place the mushies in an ovenproof dish, drizzle with oil, add the garlic, thyme and seasoning, then roast for about 8 minutes, until soft.

To serve, sit a mush on top of a rosti, cover with cheese, place under a preheated grill and grill until melted and golden. Nice served with a bit of tomato chutney.

Baigan tamatar

If you are looking for something delicious to dip your bread in, or an alternative to salsa for those addictive tortilla chips, well look no further – this aubergine and tomato dish is so delicious. I like to crank up the chilli powder to let people know I'm a serious chilli player. Are you?

Serves (8)

oil for frying

2 onions, sliced

1 garlic clove, crushed

pinch chilli powder

1 bay leaf

pinch cinnamon

pinch garam masala

450g/14½oz tomatoes, roughly chopped

450g/14½oz aubergine, cubed

50g/2oz tomato purée

salt

fresh coriander to serve

Heat the oil in a frying pan and brown the onions. You want them golden and caramelized, not burnt. This will take about 30 minutes on a low heat. Add the garlic, chilli powder, bay leaf, cinnamon, garam masala and salt. Cook for 3 minutes, then add the tomatoes and bring to the boil. Boil for 5 minutes.

Add the aubergine and tomato purée then simmer, part-covered, for 30 minutes. Season well and top with coriander, then get dipping.

Puds

Damson bread-and-butter pud

The Lythe Valley in Cumbria has the most amazing damsons. These fellas in a bread-and-butter pud are immense – use them if you can get hold of them, but blueberries will work well too if you can't.

Serves (6)

¾ loaf white bread, thin-sliced with crusts removed

200g/7oz butter

200g/7oz demerara sugar

150g/5oz damsons or blueberries

500ml/17fl oz double cream

6 eggs, 3 whole and 3 yolks only, beaten

1 vanilla pod, scraped

100g/3½oz caster sugar

extra cream to serve

Butter the bread, then cut the slices in half to make triangles. Grease and sugar a 30 x 20cm/12 x 8in ovenproof dish, then fill it up – don't cram it full, but the slices should fit snugly – layering until you have used all the bread, then put in a layer of sugar then damsons, finishing with a layer of sugar.

Heat the cream to scalding then pour on to the beaten eggs and mix in the vanilla seeds and sugar. Pour over the pud. Leave to stand for at least 30 minutes.

Preheat the oven to 180°C/350°F/Gas Mark 4. Stand the pud in a roasting tin of water and cook for 40 minutes, until the custard sets.

Serve with pouring cream.

Chocolate pancakes with chestnut cream

This looks like a child's pud, but has a really grown-up taste, due to the rum and earthy chestnuts. However, if you do want to make it for the kids, the pancakes served with banana, cream and non-boozy chocolate sauce are a massive hit with my two, Hamish and Florence.

Serves ④ (makes 8 pancakes)

Pancakes
175g/6oz self-raising flour
1 tsp bicarbonate of soda
50g/2oz sugar
25g/1oz cocoa powder
50g/2oz butter, melted
250ml/8fl oz milk
1 egg
oil for frying

Chestnut cream
250ml/8fl oz whipping cream, lightly whipped
1 vanilla pod, scraped
200g/7oz vacuum-packed chestnuts
1 tbsp icing sugar

Chocolate sauce
250ml/8fl oz water
200g/7oz dark chocolate (70% cocoa-solids)
50ml/2fl oz dark rum
25g/1oz sugar
25g/1oz butter

To make the pancakes, mix together in one bowl the flour, bicarb, sugar and cocoa. In a separate bowl, combine the butter, milk and egg, then mix the wet ingredients into the dry ones. Make the pancakes by spooning some of the mix into a hot oiled pan and cooking for about 1 minute on each side. Keep warm.

For the chestnut cream, add the vanilla seeds to the cream, then blend the chestnuts with the sugar until smooth and mix into the cream.

For the sauce, just bring the water, chocolate, rum and sugar to the boil, then simmer for 5 minutes. Take it off the heat and whisk in the butter.

To serve, layer up pancake, cream, pancake and pour over the sauce.

Sticky Guinness pudding

Sticky toffee pudding never fails to sell on the menu at Greens. In its basic form it is rich, moreish and utterly irresistible, so when you add a drop of the black stuff and some sweet, sticky blackcurrant, it is certainly not going to be horrible, is it?

Serves (6)

175g/6oz stoned dates
100ml/3½fl oz water
100ml/3½fl oz Guinness
1 tsp bicarbonate of soda
50g/2oz butter
175g/6oz sugar
2 eggs, beaten
175g/6oz self-raising flour
dash vanilla extract

Sauce
100ml/3½fl oz cream
100g/3½oz butter
100g/3½oz soft dark brown sugar
splash Guiness
splash blackcurrant liqueur

lightly whipped cream to serve

Put the dates in a saucepan with the liquid and bicarb and cook slowly until they break down – this should take about 15 minutes.

Preheat the oven to 200°C/400°F/Gas Mark 6 and grease a 28 x 18cm/11 x 7in tin. Cream the butter and sugar, then add the eggs. Next add the flour and vanilla extract, spoon into the greased tin and cook for 40 minutes.

Meanwhile, make the sauce by putting the cream, butter, sugar and Guinness in a saucepan and bringing it to the boil, then adding the blackcurrant liqueur. Serve with lightly whipped cream.

Beetroot and chocolate muffins

Muffins need to be nice and moist and the beets give moisture to this mix. They also give a dark, dark colour and earthy taste, but if you didn't know, you'd never guess that there's beetroot in the cake. You can also grate courgette into the mix instead of beets.

Serves 8

225g/7½oz beetroot
75g/3oz cocoa powder
175g/6oz plain flour
2 tsp baking powder
225g/7½oz sugar
3 eggs
200ml/7fl oz corn oil

Syrup (optional)
150ml/¼ pint red wine
zest and juice 1 orange
150g/5oz sugar

whipped cream to serve

Preheat the oven to 180°C/350°F/Gas Mark 4. Wrap the beets loosely in foil and roast for about 30 minutes. Allow to cool, then peel and chop roughly. Turn the oven up to 200°C/400°F/Gas Mark 6.

Sift the cocoa, flour, baking powder and sugar into a bowl. Put the eggs, beetroot and oil in a blender and blitz until smooth. Add the beet mix to the flour. Transfer to paper cases in the holes of a muffin tin, and cook for about 20–25 minutes. Take out and cool.

If you fancy a bit of extra something with them, then make this yummy syrup to pour over. Heat the wine, zest, juice and sugar until the sugar dissolves, then simmer and reduce until you have a thickish syrup. Now stir in the orange juice.

Serve each muffin with syrup and cream (or just scoff a muffin whole, while no-one's looking).

St Honoré-style cheesecake

St Honoré is the patron saint of pastry bakers, and St Honoré gateau is a rich, gooey cake with choux pastry and fruit. Here is my cheesecake version of it, which looks fantastic and is well worth the effort, I promise.

Serves ⑧–①②

Choux pastry

175g/6oz butter

150ml/¼ pint water

200g/7oz plain flour

6 eggs

whipped cream to fill the choux buns

Cheesecake

225g/7½oz crushed chocolate digestive

175g/6oz butter, melted

200g/7oz chocolate (70% cocoa-solids)

1kg/2lb cream cheese

200g/7oz ricotta cheese

6 eggs

150g/5oz sugar

splash rum

Chocolate sauce

150g/5oz sugar

150g/5oz butter

splash vanilla extract

150g/5oz chocolate (70% cocoa-solids)

150ml/¼ pint cold water

fresh fruit, such as raspberries, banana, mango, strawberries, soaked in rum, chopped if large

First make the choux buns. Preheat the oven to 200°C/400°F/Gas Mark 6 and grease and/or line a baking sheet. Heat the butter and water in a saucepan until the butter melts, then take off the heat and tip in the flour. Mix well then add the eggs one at a time and beat really well. Put in a piping bag and pipe small choux buns (about 2.5cm/1in blobs) on to the baking sheet. Cook for 15–20 minutes until dry and hollow. I like to put them on the bottom shelf for another 5–10 minutes to really dry them out. Cool on a wire rack, slit open and fill with whipped cream. Turn the oven down to 180°C/350°F/Gas Mark 4.

Meanwhile, make the cake. Combine the biscuit crumbs and butter and press on to the base of a 22cm/9in springform tin. Melt the chocolate in a bowl over barely simmering water. Blitz the cheeses, eggs and sugar, then add the chocolate and rum. Spoon into the tin, smooth the top and cook in the oven for 1 hour.

For the sauce, heat the sugar, butter and vanilla extract in a saucepan until they form a smooth sauce. Add the chocolate and stir gently until it melts. Gradually add the water and cook for 10 minutes.

To serve, sit the filled choux buns around the top of the cheesecake. Fill the middle with the rum-soaked fruit and pour over loads of the sauce.

Rhubarb and ginger custard tart

Here is another pud that's lovely when served as an individual portion, but is just as tasty as a big tart. Between you and me, if you make this out of season, canned rhubarb works in it rather well.

Serves (8)

Pastry
175g/6oz plain flour
75g/3oz caster sugar
75g/3oz butter
1 egg

Filling
275g/9oz rhubarb, cut into chunks
75g/3oz butter
100g/3½oz sugar

Custard
2.5cm/1 inch piece of ginger, peeled and chopped
4 egg yolks
65g/2½oz sugar
500ml/17fl oz double cream

whipped cream to serve

To make the pastry, pulse all the ingredients together in a processor, wrap and chill for half an hour. Preheat the oven to 180°C/350°F/Gas Mark 4 and roll out the pastry to fit a 22cm/9in loose-bottomed tart case. Bake blind for 15–20 minutes then allow to cool.

Melt the butter in a frying pan, add the rhubarb and sugar and cook until the fruit is soft, but not turned to mush. Allow it to cool.

To make the custard, first squeeze the juice out of the ginger by putting the pieces in a clean piece of muslin and squeezing hard over a cup. Next, whisk the yolks and sugar together, then whisk in the cream and ginger juice.

Preheat the oven to 150°C/300°F/Gas Mark 2. Place the rhubarb in the centre of the case, leaving a small gap all the way round, then pour over the custard. Bake for 30 minutes until set. Serve a good old wedge of this scrummy pud with a dollop of cream.

Three-chocolate terrine

I've had this recipe, or versions of it, in my portfolio for a very long time.
I think it is a bit old fashioned these days, but, every time I make it I love it
and I don't care that it looks a bit dated – I bet you've all got things in your
wardrobe like that.

Serves ⑥

Cake layer
50g/2oz butter
1 egg
100g/3½oz sugar
25g/1oz cocoa powder
dash vanilla extract
25g/1oz plain flour

White chocolate layer
1 tsp gelatine
100ml/3½fl oz cold water
30g/1½oz liquid glucose
225g/7½oz white chocolate, chopped
2 egg yolks
300ml/½ pint whipping cream, lightly whipped

Plain chocolate layer
1 tsp gelatine
35ml/1½fl oz cold water
150g/5oz plain chocolate
2 eggs, separated
35ml/1½fl oz rum
100ml/3½fl oz cream, lightly whipped

extra cream to serve

First make the cake: preheat the oven to 180°C/ 350°F/Gas Mark 4 and grease a 20cm/8in square tin. Melt the butter over a low heat. Whisk the egg and sugar together in a bowl, stir in the cocoa and melted butter, adding a dash of vanilla. Sift in the flour and mix. Pour into the tin and bake for 20 minutes. Allow to cool slightly, then turn on to a wire rack to cool.

Line a 1kg/2lb loaf tin with clingfilm, then cut a piece of cake to fit and put it on the bottom.

To make the white chocolate layer, put the gelatine and 35ml/1½fl oz of the water in a cup. Place this cup inside one containing hot water for 5 minutes to dissolve the gelatine. Put the remaining water and the liquid glucose in a pan and bring to the boil. Remove from the heat and stir in the chocolate and gelatine. When cooled, stir in the egg yolks. Fold in the cream and spread on top of the cake layer in the loaf tin.

Repeat the gelatine step for the plain chocolate layer. Melt the chocolate over barely simmering water in a bowl (make sure the water doesn't touch the bottom of the bowl). Stir in the egg yolks and rum while still hot. Add the gelatine. Whisk the egg whites until stiff. Fold into the chocolate, then fold in the cream.

Spoon on to the other layers and level off. Cover with clingfilm and chill for at least 8 hours. Lift the terrine out by the clingfilm and serve large slices with cream.

Toffee, banana and pecan crumble-pie

I think this completely childish dessert is for when a) you need cheering up b) you're meeting up with old friends and c) it is Tuesday. You can, of course, make little individual ones of these for a bit more of a grown-up pudding.

Serves ⑥

200g/7oz can condensed milk
225g/7½oz puff pastry
225g/7½oz plain flour
125g/4oz butter
100g/3½oz demerara sugar
50g/2oz pecan nuts, crushed
8 bananas

clotted cream to serve

To make the toffee, boil the unopened can of condensed milk for 3 hours in a large pan of water, being careful not to let it boil dry. Leave to cool. Meanwhile, preheat the oven to 180°C/350°F/Gas Mark 4 and grease a 22cm/9in tin. Roll out the pastry to fit the tin and bake it blind for 15–20 minutes.

Preheat the oven to 200°C/400°F/Gas Mark 6. Prepare the crumble top by rubbing the flour and butter together in a bowl until it forms crumbs, then add the sugar and the nuts. Chop the bananas and put them in the case, top with the toffee, and then the crumble. Cook in the oven for 15–20 minutes.

Serve the pie with loads of clotted cream.

Bakewell tart

When I was a kid I couldn't resist those cherry bakewells Mr Kipling used to make in his kitchen (he did, didn't he?). Anyway, now I'm a grown up I love traditional Bakewell tart and just that little bit of lemon zest makes it special.

Serves (8)

Pastry
300g/10oz plain flour
125g/4oz butter
30g/1½oz sugar
1 egg
a little milk to bind

Filling
225g/7½oz butter
225g/7½oz sugar
200g/7oz ground almonds
3 eggs
zest 1 lemon, finely grated
50g/2oz plain flour

1 egg, beaten, to glaze
lots of cherry jam
flaked almonds to top

For the pastry, pulse all the ingredients in a food processor, except the milk, then add a little milk to bind; wrap and chill for 1 hour. Roll out the pastry to fit a 20cm/8in tart case and chill for 20 minutes. While it is chilling, preheat the oven to 180°C/350°F/Gas Mark 4. Fill with baking beads and bake the case blind for 20 minutes. Remove the beads, brush with eggwash and cook for a couple of minutes more to set. Leave the oven on.

Meanwhile, make the filling. Cream the butter and sugar until nice and pale. Mix in the almonds, then add the eggs one at a time to the butter mix. Don't worry if they begin to split – just add a little of the flour. Now add the zest and flour.

Spread the jam generously across the base, leaving a good 2.5cm/1 inch gap around edge. Add the filling and top with flaked almonds. Cook at 180°C/350°F/Gas Mark 4 for about 20 minutes until set and golden.

Coffee, choccy and cardamom cake

This is a very rich, very fragrant cake, which I love as an Afternoon Tea kind of cake, rather than a pudding. So next time you want to imagine a bit of civilized Eastern promise, get the cardamoms out and get baking.

Serves ⑥

400ml/14fl oz milk

12 cardamom pods, crushed a little

1 heaped tsp instant coffee

30g/1½oz sugar

350g/11½oz chocolate (70% cocoa-solids)

750ml/1¼ pints double cream

toasted flaked almonds to decorate

Line a 20cm/8in deep cake tin. Put the milk and cardamom in a heavy-bottomed saucepan and bring slowly to the boil, then simmer gently to reduce by one-third. Strain off the pods and add the coffee and sugar.

Melt the chocolate in a bowl over a pan of gently simmering water. Whip the cream until it just begins to thicken. Now fold the chocolate into the cream. Add the milky coffee mix and combine.

Spoon into the tin and chill for at least 2 hours, but preferably overnight. Decorate with flaked almonds and eat with strong, sweet Turkish coffee.

Granny's cake

This isn't my granny's cake, but comes from the granny of a former neighbour. It is another recipe from my mum's repetoire and I get one of these made for me every Christmas and birthday. It is great with loads of butter.

Serves (6)

450g/14½oz self-raising flour
1 tsp baking powder
1 tsp mixed spice
pinch salt
125g/4oz sugar
125g/4oz butter
450g/14½oz mixed fruit and peel
1 tsp bicarbonate of soda
250ml/8fl oz milk

Line and grease a 1kg/2lb loaf tin. Preheat the oven to 150°C/300°F/Gas Mark 2. In a large bowl, sift together the flour, baking powder, mixed spice and salt, then add the sugar. Rub in the butter, then fold in the fruit. Mix the bicarb with the milk, then add this to the dry ingredients and mix well.

Scoop the mix into the loaf tin and cook in the oven for 2 hours. Cool … a little … then turn out and get stuck in.

Juicy lemon pudding with rich lemon sauce

Do you remember sponge pudding and/or upside-down pudding? Well, this is a sort of hybrid of the two: a fluffy sponge with a rich, zingy lemon sauce. You can make this as one pudding or in individual bowls, which is nice.

Serves (4)

Pudding
2 eggs, separated
50g/2oz butter
zest and juice 1 lemon
75g/3oz sugar
175g/6oz plain flour
150ml/¼ pint milk

Sauce
1 egg, beaten
225g/7½oz sugar
juice and zest 2 lemons
15g/½oz butter

cream to serve

Preheat the oven to 180°C/350°F/Gas Mark 4. To make the pudding, whisk the egg whites in a bowl until they are nice and stiff. In a separate bowl, cream the butter, zest and sugar until pale and fluffy. Add the yolks, flour and lemon juice, and mix it up well. Gradually add the milk, stirring all the time. Gently fold in the stiff egg whites, then spoon into a greased 600ml/1 pint pudding bowl or 4 individual bowls, and cover with foil. Stand the bowl/s in a roasting tin of water and cook in the oven for 40 minutes, or 20–25 minutes if making small ones. Turn out when done.

Meanwhile make the sauce. Heat the egg, sugar and lemon zest and juice in a saucepan, stirring occasionally until they begin to thicken. Add the butter and keep stirring until it melts and the sauce thickens.

Spoon the sauce over a generous portion of pud and serve with some cream.

Plum and ginger trifle

Well, my mum has made me a trifle-a-holic. Every Christmas, and indeed at any family gathering, she brings her legendary trifle to the party. I'm sure that's a tradition lots of you will share, so at the next big do you are going to, why not try this scary, yummy, boozy, moreish, irresistible pud?

Serves at least ⑧

400g/13oz fresh plums, pitted

200g/7oz sugar

1 tsp star anise powder

1 cinnamon stick

1 sticky ginger cake (about 400g/13oz), cut into chunks

good glug dark Jamaican rum

175g/6oz apricot jam

Custard

6 egg yolks

125g/4oz sugar

50g/2oz plain flour

2.5cm/1 inch piece of ginger, peeled and chopped

400ml/14fl oz milk

200ml/7fl oz whipped cream

Topping

300ml/½ pint whipped cream

75g/3oz crystalized ginger, finely chopped

cinnamon powder

Stew the plums, sugar, anise and cinnamon in a saucepan until the plums soften a bit, but don't disintegrate completely.

To make the custard, put the yolks, sugar and flour in a bowl and beat together. Squeeze the juice out of the ginger by putting the pieces in a clean piece of muslin and squeezing hard over a cup. Pour the milk into a heavy-bottomed saucepan and bring just up to the boil with the ginger juice. Now pour on to the egg mix, beat well, then put back on the heat until it is thick enough to coat the back of a spoon. Cover and chill. When it is really cold, fold in the whipped cream.

To make up the trifle, put the cake in the bottom of a large dish, glug on the booze and spoon over the fruit. Add about 50ml/2fl oz of water to the jam and warm slightly to soften before spreading it over the fruit. Next, spoon on the custard, top with whipped cream and decorate in a fantastically arty way with ginger pieces and a dusting of cinnamon…or hundreds and thousands if you fancy.

Chocolate and plum pudding

I love puddings with a surprise. Maybe it all goes back to the sixpence in the Christmas pudding. So I love these beauties, which are are both delicious and hide a tasty secret.

Serves ④

8 plums
pinch cinnamon
225g/7½oz sugar
100g/3½oz butter
3 eggs, 2 whole, 1 yolk only
200g/7oz self-raising flour
50g/2oz cocoa powder

Preheat the oven to 200°C/400°F/Gas Mark 6. Grease and flour 4 dariole moulds or small pudding bowls.

Place the plums, cinnamon and 75g/3oz of the sugar in a pan over low heat and cook until the plums break down. Meanwhile, cream the butter and remaining sugar until pale and fluffy. Next, beat in the 2 eggs then the yolk, one at a time. Quickly fold in the flour and the cocoa.

Spoon one-eighth of the mix into each mould, then place 2 plum pieces on top, then spoon on the remaining mix. Cover each pud with foil. Stand the moulds or bowls in a roasting tin of water and cook for 25 minutes.

Serve with crème frâiche, clotted cream, pouring cream, chocolate sauce or ice cream. You choose.

Cherry loaf

**Cup of tea, piece of cake, roaring fire, Sunday papers ... afternoon nap.
Am I getting old or are my kids still very young?**

Serves (8)

150g/5oz self-raising flour

½ tsp baking powder

75g/3oz dried cherries, plus extra
to decorate

75g/3oz glace cherries, plus extra
to decorate

100g/3½oz butter

100g/3½oz sugar

2 eggs

50ml/2fl oz sweet sherry

Icing

25g/1oz butter

125g/4oz icing sugar

splash sherry

Preheat the oven to 200°C/400°F/Gas Mark 6. Line
and grease a 20 x 7cm/8 x 3in loaf tin. Sift together
the flour and baking powder, then stir in the cherries.

In another bowl, beat the butter and sugar until really
pale (an electric whisk is good for this). Now add the
eggs and beat again. Quickly fold the flour mix into
the buttery one, then add the sherry.

Spoon into the loaf tin and and bake for 35 minutes.
Make the icing by whisking together the butter, icing
sugar and sherry in a small bowl. Smooth this over
the top and sprinkle some chopped bits of both types
of cherries over the top.

Cartmel-inspired sticky toffee cheesecake

Now, the village of Cartmel in Cumbria, just down the road from where my fab friends Dave and Christine live, is the birthplace of sticky toffee pudding, no matter what anybody else might tell you. So, my house is now the official birthplace of sticky toffee cheesecake.

Serves (8)

Base
250g/8oz ginger biscuits, crushed
175g/6oz butter

Topping
175g/6oz stoned dates
1 tsp bicarbonate of soda
200ml/7fl oz water
750g/1½lb ricotta
500g/1lb cream cheese
150g/5oz sugar
1 vanilla pod, scraped
6 eggs

Sauce
100g/3½oz butter
100g/3½oz soft dark brown sugar
100g/3½oz golden syrup
100ml/3½fl oz cream
100g/3½oz Medjool dates, chopped

Decoration
mint sprigs
200g/7oz mascarpone
1 vanilla pod
75g/3oz icing sugar

To make the base, melt the butter in a saucepan and stir in the biscuit crumbs. Press into either a 20cm/8in springform tin or 8 individual cheesecake tins.

For the topping: in a saucepan, gently heat the dates, bicarb and water until the dates break down to a thick toffee-like consistency. Allow to cool.

Preheat the oven to 180°C/350°F/Gas Mark 4. In a food processor, blend the cheeses, sugar, vanilla seeds, eggs and date mixture until smooth. Now spoon on top of the base/s and cook for about 1 hour for a large cake or 40 minutes for the small ones.

To make the sauce, put all the ingredients except the dates in a saucepan and bring up to the boil then boil for 3–4 minutes, take off the heat and fold in the dates.

Blend the mascarpone with the vanilla and icing and serve with each slice or individual cake, topped with lashings of sauce and a sprig of mint.

Date and banana scones

There is nothing more enjoyable than sitting in a swanky hotel having proper afternoon tea. In Bangkok, it is a really competitive market, with all the hotels offering magnificent buffets, all accompanied by impeccable waitress service. So make the cucumber sandwiches, get the kettle on and shimmy in that pinny as you serve up some of my delicious scones.

Makes (8)-(1)(0) scones

225g/7½oz self-raising flour

1 tsp baking powder

50g/2oz caster sugar

50g/2oz butter

1 egg

about 150ml/¼ pint milk to bind

100g/3½oz Medjool dates, chopped

2 bananas, sliced

clotted cream and apricot jam to serve

Preheat the oven to 200°C/400°F/Gas Mark 6. Sift the flour and baking powder into a bowl, and add the sugar. Rub in the butter, then mix in the egg. Add the milk and the dates and banana and mix to form a dough.

Roll out the dough to 2.5cm/1 inch thick and cut into 7cm/3in rounds. Bake these in the oven on a greased baking tray for 10 minutes. Remove and serve filled with clotted cream and apricot jam.

Banana and pistachio fool

Fools are the easiest pud in the world to make and you can use whatever flavour you fancy: chocolate, strawberry, mango. This is a rather moreish one. If you fancy it, soak the bananas in the booze for 20 minutes or so before folding them into the fool.

Serves ⑥

500ml/17fl oz whipped cream

250ml/8fl oz thick Greek yogurt

1 vanilla pod, scraped

100g/3½oz icing sugar, sieved

dash banana liqueur

200g/7oz pistachios, lightly crushed

6 bananas, sliced

Combine the cream, yogurt, vanilla and sugar to make a thick mousse-like mixture. Fold in the booze, and half the nuts and the fruit. Spoon into sundae glasses and top with the rest of the nuts.

Magic pudding

There's millions of runny centred pudds in restaurants and supermarkets these days. Don't get me wrong, I love 'em too, but this is one delicious, gooey, chocolate, fudgey pudding. It looks like it'll never work when you pour on the milk ... but, as if by magic, a pudding appears.

Serves (6)

225g/7½oz butter, melted

2 eggs, beaten

35ml/1½fl oz strong espresso coffee

575ml/18fl oz milk

350g/11½oz soft dark brown sugar

175g/6oz sifted self-raising flour

50g/2oz cocoa powder

100g/3½oz pecans

75g/3oz raisins, soaked in 75ml/3fl oz dark rum

30g/1½oz golden syrup

Sauce

300ml/½ pint double cream

50g/2oz sugar

1 vanilla pod, seeds scraped

100g/3½oz pink marshmallows

Mix the butter, eggs, coffee and 125ml/4fl oz of the milk. Now add 225g/7½oz of the sugar, the flour, cocoa, nuts and boozy raisins. Stir well. Spoon into a 1.5 litre/ 2½ pint ovenproof dish (a big soufflé dish is ideal).

Preheat the oven to 160°C/325°F/Gas Mark 3. Bring the rest of milk to scalding point in a saucepan. Add the syrup and stir to dissolve. Sprinkle the rest of the sugar over the pud, then do the same with the milk mix. Cook in the oven for about 50–60 minutes. The pudding should be springy on top, but will be gooey underneath.

To make the sauce, bring the cream, sugar and vanilla seeds slowly to the boil, then simmer for about 5 minutes to thicken. Take off the heat and add the marshmallows, stirring to start them melting. Serve a big dollop of pud with the yummy sauce over it.

Baked pecan and vanilla cheesecake with bananas Foster

Brennans, in New Orleans, invented Bananas Foster, named after the MD. It is basically bananas, booze and sugar, and is completely divine. Part two is the rather classic baked pecan cheesecake, as eaten all over the US of A. So, in summary, two of my favourites, on the same plate. Am I good to you, or what?

Makes ④ individual cakes or ① 12cm/5in cake

Base
100g/3½oz digestive biscuits, crushed
50g/2oz butter, melted

Topping
400g/13oz ricotta cheese
200g/7oz cream cheese
75g/3oz sugar
3 eggs
1 vanilla pod, scraped
75g/3oz pecans, lightly crushed

Bananas Foster
50g/2oz butter
150g/5oz light brown sugar
pinch cinnamon
50ml/2fl oz banana liqueur
4 bananas, each cut into 4 pieces
50ml/2fl oz dark rum

cream to serve

Preheat the oven to 180°C/350°F/Gas Mark 4. Grease and line either 4 individual cheesecake tins or one 12cm/5in loose-bottomed one. Make the base by combining the biscuits and butter in a bowl and press into the tin/s.

Next make the topping. Combine the cheeses, sugar, eggs and vanilla in a blender until smooth. Stir in the nuts and spoon the mix on to the base/s, then bake for about 25 minutes until set if making individual cheesecakes, if making one large one cook for 50 minutes. Allow to cool and then turn out on to a plate.

To prepare the bananas Foster, heat the butter, sugar and cinnamon over a medium-high heat until the sugar dissolves. Add the banana liqueur and mix well. Place the bananas in the pan and cook gently until they begin to brown, about 3–4 minutes. Now add the rum (it should flame if the pan's hot enough) and cook for a few minutes. Spoon the Bananas Foster over each of the cheesecakes, top with cream and be amazed.

Chocolate tart

This is a real classic dessert at my restaurant, Greens. All things chocolatey sell well and this is right up there at the top of the list. It is a tart with a filling that has the texture of expensive chocolates. No wonder it is popular: nothing more to add, really.

Serves (8)

Tart case
200g/7oz plain flour
25g/1oz cocoa powder
pinch salt
100g/3½oz butter
25g/1oz sugar
1 egg
dash milk to bind, if necessary

Filling
400ml/14fl oz cream
dash vanilla extract
100g/3½oz sugar
50g/2oz butter
400g/13oz chocolate (70% cocoa-solids)

Sauce
150g/5oz sugar
150ml/¼ pint water
1 vanilla pod, scraped
400g/13oz bag frozen raspberries

whipped cream to serve

To make the tart case, pulse all the ingredients in a blender, except the milk to form a dough. Now add the milk to loosen it a touch if necessary. Roll out the dough to just larger than a 22cm/9in tart case, push it in and up the sides, trim the edges, and chill for at least 1 hour (if you roll out using a mix of flour and icing sugar on the board and rolling pin, it'll keep the pastry nice and moist). Preheat the oven to 180°C/350°F/Gas Mark 4, then bake the case blind for 25 minutes, until crisp.

To make the filling, bring the cream, vanilla and sugar to the boil. Pour over the chocolate and butter, whisk slowly until all is combined and shiny and glossy. Pour into the case and leave to set overnight in the fridge.

For the sauce, melt the sugar and water together. Add the raspberries and vanilla, remove from heat, blend and pass through a sieve.

Serve a big wedge of tart with whipped cream and the sauce.

Vodka, sultana and poppy-seed cheesecake

By now you will all know about my cheesecake obsession. Well, this is a real grown-up one. Serve this at a dinner party where your mates like to have a few bevvies (mmm, that'll be all of mine then). Charcoal crackers can be used instead of Oreo cookies to make the base.

Serves at least ① ②

Base
225g/7½oz Oreos (or charcoal crackers)
150g/5oz butter, melted
30g/1½oz icing sugar

Topping
100g/3½oz sultanas
100ml/3½fl oz lemon vodka
750g/1½lb ricotta cheese
400g/13oz cream cheese
6 eggs
150g/5oz sugar
1 vanilla pod, scraped
about 30g/1½oz poppy seeds

whipped cream and vodka to serve

First, soak the sultanas overnight in the vodka. To make the base, crush the cookies or crackers and combine with the butter and icing sugar, then press into the base of a 23cm/9¼in springform tin.

Preheat the oven to 180°C/350°F/Gas Mark 4. For the topping, blend together the cheeses, eggs, sugar and vanilla until smooth. Transfer the mixture to a bowl and fold in the drained sultanas. Spoon this on to the biscuit base. Finally, sprinkle over the poppy seeds to completely cover the top, then bake in the oven for about 1 hour. The top should still be a little wobbly in the very middle when it is done, but it'll firm up as it cools. Once it is cooled, serve with whipped cream and another shot of vodka.

Index

Numbers in *italic* indicate pictures